MONETIZING YOUR PASSION

HOW TO TURN YOUR HOBBIES INTO INCOME

DAVID SANDUA

Monetizing your passion: How to turn your hobbies into income
Paperback Edition

*"Choose a job you love,
and you will never have to work a day in your life".*

Confucius.

INDEX

I. INTRODUCTION

In today's fast-paced and competitive world, finding a balance between work and personal passions can seem like an elusive dream. What if I told you that you have the power to turn your hobbies into a source of income? Imagine waking up every morning excited to work on something you truly love, while also earning a substantial income from it. By understanding how to identify opportunities, creating a business plan and utilizing digital tools, you can successfully turn your hobbies into a lucrative career path. The first step towards monetizing your passion is to identify the opportunities within the market. Take some time to reflect on your hobbies and pinpoint areas where there may be a demand or untapped potential. For example, if you enjoy photography, you could explore various avenues such as event photography, stock photography or starting a photography blog. As you delve deeper into your hobby, it is essential to do thorough research to understand the current market trends, target audience and potential competitors. By identifying these opportunities, you gain a clear understanding of where your passion aligns with the demands of the market, setting a solid foundation for your business venture. Once you have identified the opportunities within your chosen field, the next step is to create a comprehensive business plan. A well-designed business plan serves as a roadmap for your monetization journey, outlining the steps you need to take to achieve your goals. Start by defining your business objectives, including your financial targets, marketing strategies and time frames. Consider aspects such as pricing, distribution channels and customer acquisition methods to ensure your plan is well-rounded and executable. The business plan should also include contingency measures to mitigate risks and adapt to unforeseen circumstances. By meticulously planning and strategizing, you can carve a path towards success and ensure the sustainable growth of your passion-turned-business. In today's digital age, digital tools play a crucial role in the success of any business. Utilize the power of technology to maximize the reach and impact of your monetization efforts. One such tool is social media, which allows you to showcase your work to a global audience and connect with potential customers. Build a strong online presence by creating dedicated social media accounts, sharing engaging content and actively engaging with your followers. Consider investing in a professional website or online store to showcase and sell your products or services. These digital tools not only provide exposure but also act as powerful communication channels, enabling you to directly interact with your target audience and build a loyal customer base. Monetizing your passion is not without its challenges. It requires dedication, perseverance and a willingness to adapt to changing circumstances. The rewards of pursing your hobbies and turning them into a source of income are immeasurable. Not only do you get to spend your days doing what you love, but you can also create a sustainable and fulfilling career. By identifying opportunities within your chosen field, creating a solid business plan and utilizing digital tools, you can embark on the journey of turning your passion into a profitable endeavor. So, take the leap, unleash your creativity and monetize your passion, because when you do what you love, the possibilities are endless.

THE CONCEPT OF MONETIZING HOBBIES

Monetizing hobbies is the process of turning one's personal interests and passions into a source of income. It involves identifying potential opportunities, creating a business plan and utilizing various digital tools to transform one's hobbies into a profitable endeavor. In today's rapidly evolving digital landscape, it has become increasingly accessible for individuals to monetize their hobbies, thanks to the countless platforms and technologies available. This concept holds immense value for individuals seeking to combine their passions with financial stability, as it allows them to do what they love while making money from it. The key to successfully monetizing hobbies lies in the ability to identify viable opportunities and strategically implement one's business plan. To effectively monetize hobbies, it is crucial to begin by identifying opportunities that align with one's interests and passions. This can be done by examining the current market trends, assessing the demand for specific products or services and conducting thorough research within the relevant industry. By critically analyzing these aspects, individuals can gain insights into the potential profitability of their hobbies and determine if there is a market demand that they can cater to. For instance, someone passionate about cooking may explore options such as starting a food blog, offering cooking classes or even launching their own line of cooking products. By being actively aware of the opportunities that exist within their respective fields, individuals can make informed decisions regarding the monetization of their hobbies. Once potential opportunities have been identified, it is essential to create a solid business plan that encompasses all aspects of the monetization process. A well-defined business plan outlines the goals, strategies and steps required to navigate the journey from hobby to income stream. This includes determining the target audience, setting realistic financial objectives, establishing a marketing strategy and developing a comprehensive timeline to monitor progress. A meticulously crafted business plan provides a roadmap that helps individuals stay focused and organized, ensuring that they make calculated decisions at every step of the monetization process. In today's digitally-driven world, digital tools play a pivotal role in the monetization of hobbies. By leveraging various online platforms and technologies, individuals can reach a wider audience, effectively market their products or services and optimize their overall business operations. For example, social media platforms such as Instagram and Facebook provide robust marketing opportunities for individuals to showcase their hobbies and engage with potential customers. Through captivating visual content, regular updates and effective engagement strategies, social media platforms can serve as powerful tools to attract attention and generate income. E-commerce platforms such as Shopify or Etsy offer individuals a platform to sell their products or services online, expanding their reach beyond geographical limitations. By harnessing the power of digital tools, individuals can maximize their potential to monetize their hobbies successfully. Monetizing hobbies not only allows individuals to generate income but also enables them to derive a sense of fulfillment and satisfaction from pursuing their passions. By transforming what was once a personal interest into a viable business venture, individuals can unlock a multitude of opportunities that blend their work and personal lives seamlessly. It is important to note that monetizing hobbies requires dedication, perseverance and adaptability. Building a successful business around a hobby entails continuous learning, staying abreast of industry trends and adapting to changing consumer demands. It requires individuals to constantly evolve their strategies, experiment with new approaches and be open to feedback and improvement. Monetizing hobbies is a promising avenue for individuals seeking to combine their passions with financial stability. By identifying viable opportunities, creating a comprehensive business plan and effectively utilizing digital tools, individuals can transform their hobbies into a source of income. Success in this endeavor is dependent upon thorough research, meticulous planning and the ability to adapt to ever-evolving industry landscapes. Through the monetization of hobbies, individuals can not only do what they love but also derive immense satisfaction and fulfillment from their pursuits.

PURSUING PASSIONS AND MAKING MONEY FROM THEM

One major reason why pursuing passions and making money from them is crucial is because it can lead to personal fulfillment and happiness. When individuals engage in activities that they are passionate about, they tend to feel a sense of purpose and satisfaction. This is because they are doing something that truly brings them joy and allows them to express their creativity and skills. For example, if someone has always had a passion for cooking, turning this passion into a career by opening up a restaurant can bring immense happiness and fulfillment. They will wake up every day excited to go to work, knowing that they are doing something they love and making a living out of it. This is in stark contrast to individuals who may be stuck in a job they dislike, where every day feels like a chore and they are simply working to pay the bills. In pursuing their passions and making money from them, individuals are able to live a life that is authentic to who they truly are and experience a deeper level of satisfaction and contentment. Pursuing passions and making money from them can also lead to financial stability and success. Often, individuals who are passionate about what they do are willing to invest more time, effort and resources into it, which increases their chances of success. When someone is deeply interested in a particular hobby or activity, they are more likely to stay committed and dedicated to perfecting their skills and improving their craft. This dedication can ultimately lead to recognition, opportunities and financial rewards. For example, a talented artist who is passionate about painting may start off by selling their artwork at local art shows and galleries. As they gain recognition and a following, their paintings may start selling for higher prices and they may even get commissioned for larger projects. By pursuing their passion and continuously working on their craft, they are able to turn their hobby into a lucrative business and achieve financial stability. The pursuit of passions and the ability to make money from them can also have a positive impact on society as a whole. When individuals are encouraged to pursue their passions, they often come up with innovative ideas and solutions that can address various societal needs. For example, individuals who are passionate about environmental sustainability may come up with sustainable business models or products that help reduce carbon footprints and promote eco-friendly lifestyles. By monetizing their passion, these individuals are not only able to make a living, but they are also making a positive impact on the environment and society as a whole. When individuals are engaged in activities they are passionate about, they are more likely to give back to their communities. They may use their skills and resources to support local causes or mentor others who are interested in their field. This creates a ripple effect of inspiration and positivity, benefiting society at large. The importance of pursuing passions and making money from them cannot be overstated. Not only does it lead to personal fulfillment and happiness, but it also provides financial stability and success. The pursuit of passions can have a positive impact on society by fostering innovation and addressing societal needs. So, why settle for a job that simply pays the bills when there is an opportunity to do what you love and make money from it? Whether it is turning a hobby into a business, creating a brand or using digital tools to monetize your passion, the possibilities are endless. By embracing and pursuing your passions, you can create a life that is authentic to who you truly are and make a positive impact on the world around you.

THE ESSAY'S CONTENT

In this essay, we will provide an overview of the content that will be covered, focusing on how individuals can monetize their hobbies and turn them into a source of income. The essay will start by discussing the importance of identifying opportunities within one's hobbies. It will explore the idea that every hobby has the potential to be monetized, as long as individuals can find a unique angle or niche that sets them apart from others. The essay will emphasize the need to research the market and identify areas where there is a demand for products or services related to the hobby. This will include examining trends, competition and target audience demographics. By thoroughly understanding the landscape, individuals can position themselves to take advantage of the opportunities available to them.

The essay will then delve into the process of creating a business plan, which serves as a roadmap for turning a hobby into a profitable venture. It will emphasize the importance of setting clear goals, defining target markets and designing a marketing strategy that effectively reaches potential customers. The essay will also highlight the need for financial planning, including budgeting for start-up costs, ongoing expenses and projected revenue streams. By carefully considering these aspects and developing a comprehensive business plan, individuals can increase their chances of success and ensure that their passion is sustainable in the long term. The essay will explore how digital tools can be utilized to monetize one's passion effectively. It will discuss the various platforms and technologies available that can help individuals showcase their skills, products or services to a wider audience. This will include a discussion of social media platforms, websites, e-commerce platforms and digital marketing techniques. The essay will provide guidance on how to leverage these tools effectively, such as optimizing online presence, engaging with potential customers and utilizing data analytics to make informed business decisions. By harnessing the power of digital tools, individuals can expand the reach of their hobby-based business and maximize their earning potential.

The essay will also touch on the importance of continuous learning and adaptation in the process of monetizing one's hobby. It will emphasize that the market is constantly evolving and individuals need to stay up-to-date with emerging trends and techniques. This may involve attending workshops, webinars or industry conferences to gain new skills and knowledge. Individuals will need to embrace a mindset of experimentation and innovation, continuously refining their products or services to meet evolving customer needs. By staying proactive and adaptable, individuals can ensure that their hobby-based business remains relevant and competitive. This essay will provide a comprehensive overview of how individuals can monetize their hobbies and turn them into a source of income. By identifying opportunities within their chosen passion, creating a well-thought-out business plan, utilizing digital tools effectively and embracing continuous learning and adaptation, individuals can successfully transform their passion into a sustainable and profitable venture. This essay aims to empower readers to take the first steps towards monetizing their hobbies, so they can do what they love and make money from it. To successfully monetize your passion, it is important to identify opportunities that align with your hobbies and interests. Start by conducting market research to determine what potential customers are looking for and what products or services are in demand. This will help you tailor your offerings to meet the needs of your target audience and increase your chances of success. It is crucial to stay updated on industry trends and be flexible in your approach, as market demands and customer preferences can shift over time. Once you have identified a viable opportunity, it is essential to create a solid business plan that outlines your goals, strategies and financial projections. Your business plan will serve as your roadmap and help guide your decisions and actions. It should include details about your target market, competitors, marketing strategies and pricing. It is advisable to include contingency plans to deal with potential obstacles or challenges that may arise along the way.

To monetize your passion effectively, it is essential to leverage the power of digital tools and platforms. The internet has revolutionized the way businesses operate, providing numerous opportunities for individuals to showcase their talents and sell their products or services online. Creating a strong online presence through social media platforms, online marketplaces and personal websites can significantly expand your reach and attract potential customers from all around the world. Leveraging digital marketing techniques such as search engine optimization (SEO), email marketing and influencer collaborations can help increase your visibility and generate more online sales.

In addition to utilizing digital tools, it is crucial to establish a strong brand identity that resonates with your target audience. Your brand should clearly communicate your values, aesthetic and unique selling points. It is important to consistently deliver high-quality products or services that reflect your brand's promise and build trust with your customers. Establishing a strong brand not only helps differentiate yourself from competitors but also creates a loyal customer base that will support and promote your business. Networking and collaboration are also valuable strategies to monetize your passion. Actively seek out networking opportunities, attend industry events and connect with like-minded individuals who share similar interests. Collaborating with other professionals in your field can open doors to new possibilities, expand your network and create synergistic partnerships. Consider joining professional associations or online communities related to your hobby or industry to gain valuable insights, resources and support. To ensure long-term sustainability and profitability, it is important to continuously evaluate and adapt your business strategies based on feedback and market trends. Monitor customer satisfaction, track sales and expenses and regularly review your business plan to identify areas for improvement and growth. Embrace a mindset of continuous learning and adaptability, as staying up-to-date with industry developments and incorporating customer feedback into your offering will help you stay ahead of the competition and meet evolving market demands. Turning your hobbies into income can be a fulfilling and rewarding endeavor. It allows you to do what you love while also making money from it. It requires dedication, perseverance and a strategic approach. By identifying opportunities, creating a strong business plan, leveraging digital tools, building a strong brand, networking and staying adaptable, you can successfully monetize your passion and turn it into a sustainable source of income. So take that leap of faith, invest in yourself and embark on this exciting journey to transform your hobby into a thriving business venture.

II. IDENTIFYING OPPORTUNITIES

In order to successfully monetize your passion and turn your hobbies into a source of income, it is crucial to identify the opportunities that exist in your chosen field. Opportunities can come in various forms and it is essential to be able to recognize and capitalize on them. One way to identify opportunities is by staying informed and keeping abreast of the latest trends and developments in your field of interest. By constantly staying updated, you can identify gaps in the market and find unique ways to fill them. For example, if you are passionate about photography, staying informed about the latest technological advancements in cameras and editing software can help you identify opportunities to offer photography classes or workshops to individuals who want to improve their skills. Another way to identify opportunities is by observing the needs and demands of others within your hobby or passion. Paying attention to what people within your community or social circle are seeking or struggling with can help you identify areas where you can provide value and offer your expertise. For instance, if you are passionate about baking and notice that many people around you are always on the lookout for delicious and healthy gluten-free desserts, you could start a business specializing in gluten-free baked goods. By identifying this specific need, you can position yourself as an expert in the field and meet the demands of a niche market. Networking and building connections with individuals within your field can also lead to identifying new opportunities. Attending conferences, workshops and networking events can expose you to individuals who share the same interests and passions as you. Engaging in conversations, listening to others and sharing your own ideas can help you discover potential collaborations, partnerships or business opportunities. For example, if you are a music enthusiast, connecting with fellow music lovers and professionals in the industry can open doors to opportunities such as creating a music podcast, organizing music events or even becoming a music critic. Building connections and nurturing relationships within your field can provide insights and increase your chances of discovering new opportunities. In addition to these conventional methods, utilizing digital tools and platforms can significantly help in identifying opportunities to monetize your passion. The digital age has revolutionized the way we interact and conduct business, providing countless opportunities to turn hobbies into income-generating ventures. Social media platforms such as Instagram, YouTube and TikTok offer a vast audience and potential customer base for creative individuals. By building a following and sharing quality content related to your passion, you can attract the attention of brands, sponsors or potential clients who may be interested in collaborating with you or purchasing your products. These platforms also offer valuable insights and analytics, allowing you to understand your audience better and tailor your offerings to their preferences and needs. Online marketplaces such as Etsy or Amazon provide accessible platforms to sell products or services related to your hobbies. Whether it's handmade crafts, unique artwork or digital designs, these online platforms offer an opportunity to reach a wide customer base and generate income. Identifying opportunities is a crucial step in monetizing your passion and turning your hobbies into a source of income. By staying informed, observing the needs of others, networking and utilizing digital tools, you can discover unique ways to fill gaps in the market and provide value to others. Whether it's offering specialized services, creating niche products or building a following online, identifying opportunities allows you to do what you love while making money from it. The path to monetizing your passion may not always be straightforward, but with some creativity, research and dedication, it is possible to turn your hobbies into a fulfilling and lucrative venture.

PERSONAL INTERESTS AND SKILLS

Reflecting on personal interests and skills is crucial when considering how to turn hobbies into a source of income. To successfully monetize our passion, we must first identify the skills and interests that we possess. This self-reflection allows us to evaluate our strengths and weaknesses, enabling us to make informed decisions about which avenues to pursue. Perhaps we have always loved painting, but we recognize that our skills are more suited to graphic design. By acknowledging this, we can focus our efforts on honing our skills in graphic design and explore opportunities in this field. Reflecting on personal interests helps us identify the areas in which we are most passionate. When we genuinely enjoy our work, it doesn't feel like a chore but rather a fulfilling endeavor. This passion also translates into the quality of our work, as we are more inclined to put in the time and effort necessary to excel. For instance, if we have a deep interest in photography, we are more likely to invest in high-quality equipment and dedicate ourselves to improving our craft. By aligning our interests and skills, we can ensure that we are pursuing income-generating opportunities that we are genuinely passionate about, which ultimately leads to greater success and satisfaction.

ASSESSING HOBBIES THAT HAVE POTENTIAL FOR MONETIZATION

Although many hobbies can be monetized with the proper approach, it is important to assess which hobbies have the greatest potential for generating income. One key factor to consider is the market demand for the products or services associated with the hobby. Certain hobbies may have a niche market, limiting the potential customer base and income opportunities. Hobbies that align with popular trends or markets are more likely to attract a larger customer base, increasing the potential for monetization. For example, in recent years, there has been a surge in interest in health and wellness, leading to a higher demand for yoga classes, organic products and fitness accessories. As a result, individuals with a passion for fitness and wellness may find greater success in monetizing their hobbies compared to those with less popular or mainstream hobbies. The skills and expertise required to pursue a hobby can significantly impact its potential for monetization. Hobbies that require specialized knowledge or expertise can often be more easily monetized than those that do not. For instance, someone who has developed advanced culinary skills through their passion for cooking may have the potential to offer cooking lessons or start a catering business. In contrast, a hobbyist who enjoys gardening as a pastime may face more difficulties in monetizing their interest, as it may not require the same level of expertise or offer as many viable opportunities for income generation. Thus, assessing the level of skill required can provide valuable insights into the monetization prospects of a hobby.

It is essential to consider the scalability of a hobby when assessing its potential for monetization. Some hobbies may have inherent limitations that make it difficult to scale up and generate significant income. For instance, hobbies that rely on the creation of handmade products may have a limited production capacity, thereby constraining the potential for scalability. Conversely, hobbies that lend themselves to digital platforms, such as writing or graphic design, can be easily scaled up to reach a wider audience. With the proliferation of online marketplaces and digital tools, individuals with such hobbies have the potential to earn income by selling their work or offering their services on a global scale. The scalability of a hobby should be carefully evaluated when identifying opportunities for income generation. Another important factor to consider when assessing hobbies for their potential to be monetized is the level of competition in the market. Some hobbies may have already attracted numerous individuals attempting to monetize them, leading to fierce competition and potentially diminishing the chances of success. Hobbies that are relatively untapped or in emerging markets may present greater opportunities for monetization. For instance, as the demand for sustainable and eco-friendly products continues to grow, individuals with hobbies related to upcycling or creating environmentally-conscious products may find a niche market with less competition. Considering the level of competition is crucial in determining the viability of monetizing a hobby. Assessing hobbies for their potential to generate income requires thoughtful evaluation of various factors. Understanding the market demand, the level of skill required, the scalability and the level of competition can provide valuable insights into the monetization prospects of a particular hobby. By carefully considering these factors, individuals can identify opportunities, create a business plan and leverage digital tools to turn their hobbies into a source of income. Remember, with the right approach and dedication, it is possible to do what you love and make money from it. Monetizing your passion may not only provide financial rewards but also enable you to pursue a fulfilling and purposeful career.

EVALUATING SKILLS AND KNOWLEDGE THAT CAN BE LEVERAGED

In order to successfully monetize their passion, individuals must possess the skills and knowledge necessary to identify and leverage opportunities. Evaluating these skills and knowledge is a critical step in the process of turning hobbies into income. It is essential to have a deep understanding of one's hobby or passion. This includes not only the technical aspects, but also the broader context and industry trends. For example, if someone is passionate about photography and wants to turn it into a business, they need to have expertise in various types of photography, such as portrait, nature or event photography.

They should stay updated with the latest camera equipment, editing software and trends in the photography industry to ensure they can provide value to clients and stand out from competitors. In addition to the specific skills related to the hobby itself, individuals need to evaluate their business and marketing skills. While one might excel at their hobby, turning it into a source of income requires an entirely different set of skills. For instance, individuals should possess strong organizational and time management skills to handle client bookings, keep track of expenses and meet deadlines. They should understand marketing principles and be able to create a compelling brand that attracts customers. This may involve developing a unique selling proposition, identifying target audiences and effectively utilizing social media and other digital marketing channels. By assessing their business and marketing skills, individuals can identify areas they may need to improve to ensure a successful transition from hobby to business. Individuals need to have a realistic understanding of the market demand and competition within their chosen industry. Even if someone is extremely passionate and skilled in their hobby, it does not guarantee immediate success. Conducting market research is crucial to identify opportunities and assess the viability of monetizing a particular passion. This research may involve analyzing competitors, understanding customer preferences and behavior and identifying gaps in the market that can be filled. By evaluating the market demand and competition, individuals can make informed decisions and develop strategies to position themselves effectively in the market. Individuals should assess their networking and communication skills. Building a successful business often requires collaborating with others, whether it be partners, suppliers or clients. Individuals should have the ability to connect with people, build relationships and effectively communicate their ideas and value proposition. This may involve attending industry events, joining relevant associations and actively engaging in networking opportunities. By evaluating their networking and communication skills, individuals can work on strengthening these abilities and expanding their professional network, which can be instrumental in monetizing their passion. Individuals should consider their financial literacy and budgeting skills. Turning hobbies into income may involve significant investments in equipment, marketing and other resources. Individuals should have a solid understanding of financial concepts and be able to develop a comprehensive business plan that includes forecasting expenses, setting pricing strategies and projecting revenue. They should also be proficient in budgeting to ensure they have a clear overview of their finances and can make informed decisions to sustain and grow their business in the long run.

Successfully monetizing one's passion requires a thorough evaluation of the skills and knowledge that can be leveraged. This includes a deep understanding of the chosen hobby or passion, as well as the broader industry trends and context. Individuals should assess their business and marketing skills, as well as their networking and communication abilities, to ensure they can effectively position themselves in the market and attract customers. Financial literacy and budgeting skills are essential for developing a sustainable business plan and managing resources effectively. By evaluating these skills and knowledge, individuals can determine their strengths and areas for improvement, enabling them to confidently embark on the journey of turning their hobbies into a source of income.

RESEARCHING NICHE MARKETS AND TARGET AUDIENCES

In addition to identifying opportunities and creating a business plan, another crucial step in monetizing your passion is researching niche markets and target audiences. Niche markets refer to specific segments of the population that have unique needs and preferences. By targeting niche markets, entrepreneurs can avoid competing with large corporations and increase their chances of success by offering specialized products or services. To effectively reach these niche markets, it is essential to conduct thorough research and understand the needs, wants and behaviors of their target audience. One effective way to research niche markets is to conduct market research surveys. Surveys provide valuable insights into consumer preferences, behaviors and trends, allowing entrepreneurs to make data-driven decisions. By asking specific questions, entrepreneurs can gain a deeper understanding of their target audience and identify market gaps that can be exploited. For example, a survey could ask respondents about their purchasing habits, their preferred brands and their willingness to pay for a particular product or service. Through these surveys, entrepreneurs can gain insights into their target audience's motivation and tailor their offerings to meet their needs more effectively. Another useful research tool is social media listening. With the advent of social media platforms, individuals and businesses now have access to vast amounts of data about consumer behavior. By monitoring social media conversations and analyzing user-generated content, entrepreneurs can gain valuable insights about their target audience's preferences and behaviors. For example, by analyzing hashtags and keywords associated with their niche market, entrepreneurs can identify trends, popular products or services and influencers that can help promote their business. Social media listening allows entrepreneurs to gather feedback and engage with their target audience, building loyal and long-lasting relationships.

Entrepreneurs can leverage online analytics tools to gather data and gain insights into their target audience's online behavior. Tools such as Google Analytics or Facebook Insights provide valuable information about website traffic, user demographics and engagement metrics. By analyzing this data, entrepreneurs can identify the source of their online traffic, understand their audience's preferences and optimize their online presence accordingly. For instance, if the majority of their online traffic comes from a specific social media platform, entrepreneurs can focus their marketing efforts on that platform and tailor their messaging to resonate with that particular audience. Entrepreneurs should consider conducting competitor analysis to understand their niche market better. By examining their competitors' marketing strategies, pricing models and customer reviews, entrepreneurs can gain valuable insights into their target audience's preferences and expectations. This knowledge can be used to differentiate their products or services and offer a unique value proposition. For instance, if a competitor is known for their poor customer service, an entrepreneur can highlight their exceptional customer support as a unique selling point, appealing to dissatisfied customers in the niche market. Entrepreneurs should not overlook the importance of staying updated with industry trends and market research reports. By keeping track of emerging trends and industry developments, entrepreneurs can identify new opportunities and potential threats to their business. Market research reports provide valuable insights and data about specific industries, allowing entrepreneurs to make informed decisions. For example, if a market research report indicates a growing demand for organic skincare products, an entrepreneur passionate about skincare can capitalize on this trend by offering a range of organic and sustainable skincare products.

Researching niche markets and target audiences is a crucial step in monetizing your passion. By conducting market research surveys, leveraging social media listening, using online analytics tools and conducting competitor analysis, entrepreneurs can gain valuable insights into their target audience's preferences and behaviors. Staying updated with industry trends and market research reports enables entrepreneurs to identify opportunities and make informed decisions. By thoroughly researching niche markets and understanding their target audience, entrepreneurs can tailor their offerings, increase their chances of success and ultimately monetize their passion.

IDENTIFYING EXISTING DEMAND FOR SPECIFIC PRODUCTS OR SERVICES

Identifying existing demand for specific products or services is a crucial step in monetizing one's hobbies. Without understanding the market and the needs of potential customers, it can be challenging to create a successful business plan and generate income from one's passion. Market research and analysis are essential in determining if there is a demand for the products or services one intends to offer. One way to identify existing demand is by conducting thorough market research. This involves gathering data and information about the target market, competitors and customer preferences. Market research provides valuable insights and helps determine if there is a need for the products or services one intends to offer. By analyzing trends, consumer behavior and competitors' strategies, entrepreneurs can gain a better understanding of the market's existing demand. In addition to conducting market research, it is important to consider the specific niche or target audience for one's products or services. Understanding the unique needs and preferences of a particular group can help entrepreneurs tailor their offerings accordingly. By identifying a niche market, individuals can target a specific group of customers who are likely to have a higher demand for their products or services. One effective digital tool for identifying existing demand is social media platforms. These platforms can provide valuable insights into consumer behavior and preferences. By analyzing engagement metrics, such as likes, comments and shares, entrepreneurs can gauge the interest and demand for specific products or services. Social media also allows individuals to interact directly with potential customers, gather feedback and build a loyal customer base. The use of online surveys and polls is another effective way to identify existing demand. These tools allow entrepreneurs to gather feedback from potential customers and determine their preferences and needs. By asking targeted questions related to the products or services one intends to offer, individuals can gain insights into what customers are looking for. Online surveys and polls can be shared on social media, emailed to potential customers or posted on relevant online platforms.

Another strategy for identifying existing demand is by observing industry trends and staying updated with market news. Entrepreneurs should closely follow their industry to identify emerging trends and changing consumer preferences. This information can help them adapt their offerings to meet the current and future demands of the market. By staying informed, individuals can position themselves as experts in their field and provide innovative solutions that meet the evolving needs of customers.

Entrepreneurs can also seek feedback from friends, family and trusted individuals who have experience in the industry. Their insights and perspectives can provide valuable feedback and help identify any gaps or opportunities in the market. By leveraging the knowledge and expertise of others, individuals can refine their business ideas and ensure that they are meeting existing demand. Attending industry conferences, trade shows and networking events can provide valuable opportunities to meet potential customers and industry professionals. These events allow entrepreneurs to showcase their products or services, gather feedback and establish valuable connections. By engaging with industry professionals and potential customers, individuals can gather insights that will help them further refine their offerings and identify existing demand. Identifying existing demand for specific products or services is essential when turning hobbies into a source of income. Conducting market research, identifying a niche market, leveraging digital tools, staying updated with industry trends, seeking feedback from trusted individuals and attending industry events are all effective strategies for identifying existing demand. By understanding the needs and preferences of potential customers, entrepreneurs can develop products or services that meet the market demand and successfully monetize their passions.

ANALYZING COMPETITORS AND FINDING UNIQUE SELLING POINTS

Analyzing competitors and finding unique selling points are crucial steps in the process of turning your hobbies into a source of income. In order to effectively monetize your passion, it is essential to understand the competitive landscape and what sets you apart from others in the market. By conducting a thorough analysis of your competitors, you can gain valuable insights into their strategies, strengths and weaknesses. This information will help you identify gaps in the market and determine how you can position yourself uniquely. One way to analyze your competitors is by conducting a SWOT analysis. This involves evaluating the strengths, weaknesses, opportunities and threats of each competitor in your industry. By identifying their strengths, you can gain an understanding of what they are doing well and determine how you can differentiate yourself. For example, if a competitor is known for their exceptional customer service, you can focus on providing a personalized and tailored experience for your customers. By identifying their weaknesses, you can pinpoint areas where you can capitalize and excel. For instance, if a competitor lacks a strong online presence, you can leverage digital tools to reach a wider audience and gain a competitive edge. Analyzing your competitors also allows you to identify opportunities in the market that have not yet been tapped into. By understanding what your competitors are not offering, you can fill this gap and provide a unique value proposition to your customers. For example, if you notice that none of your competitors are offering eco-friendly products or services, you can position yourself as a sustainable alternative and attract customers who prioritize environmental consciousness. This will not only set you apart from your competitors but also appeal to a growing segment of conscious consumers. Another effective method of analyzing competitors is by conducting market research. By staying updated on industry trends, consumer preferences and emerging technologies, you can gain a competitive advantage. This research will allow you to identify the current needs and desires of your target market and tailor your products or services to meet these demands. For example, if you discover that there is a rising demand for personalized fitness programs, you can develop unique offerings that cater to this specific need. This knowledge will enable you to position yourself as an expert in the field and attract customers who are seeking specialized solutions.

In addition to analyzing your competitors, it is equally important to identify and leverage your unique selling points. What sets you apart from others in the market? What makes your hobby or passion distinctive? By answering these questions, you can craft a compelling value proposition that resonates with your target audience. For instance, if you are a photographer, your unique selling point could be your ability to capture authentic and candid moments that truly reflect the essence of your subjects. This can differentiate you from photographers who focus primarily on posed and staged shots. Another way to identify your unique selling points is by tapping into your own personal story and experiences. What led you to pursue this hobby or passion? How has it shaped you as an individual? By sharing your personal journey and the reasons behind your passion, you can connect with your audience on a deeper level. People are often drawn to authenticity and by showcasing your genuine enthusiasm and expertise, you can establish a strong rapport with your customers. Analyzing competitors and finding unique selling points are crucial steps in monetizing your passion. By conducting a SWOT analysis and market research, you can gain insights into the competitive landscape and identify gaps in the market. By leveraging your unique selling points, you can differentiate yourself from others in the industry and attract customers who resonate with your value proposition. With careful analysis and a clear understanding of what makes you unique, you can successfully turn your hobbies into a sustainable source of income.

Turning your hobbies into a source of income can be an exciting and rewarding journey. Not only does it allow you to pursue your passions, but it also gives you the opportunity to make money doing what you love. It's important to approach this endeavor with careful planning and consideration. In order to successfully monetize your hobbies, you need to first identify the opportunities available to you. One way to identify opportunities is to take a step back and evaluate your hobbies and interests. Consider what skills and expertise you have developed through your hobbies and how you can translate them into a marketable product or service. For example, if you enjoy photography, you could start a photography business or sell your prints online. If you're a skilled baker, you could start a home-based bakery or sell your goods at local markets. By identifying the skills and knowledge you have acquired through your hobbies, you can begin to see how they can be monetized. Once you have identified potential opportunities, it's important to create a business plan. This plan will serve as a roadmap for your journey towards monetizing your hobbies. Start by defining your goals and objectives. What do you hope to achieve by turning your hobbies into a source of income? Do you want to build a full-time business or simply earn some extra cash on the side? Next, outline your target market. Who are your potential customers? What are their needs and preferences? Understanding your target market will allow you to tailor your products or services to their desires. Your business plan should include a marketing strategy. How will you promote your products or services? Will you use social media, website advertising or word-of-mouth? By carefully considering these elements and putting them down on paper, you can increase your chances of success. In today's digital age, it's essential to utilize digital tools to monetize your passions. The internet offers a plethora of opportunities for individuals looking to turn their hobbies into income. One way to do this is by creating an online presence. Build a website or blog where you can showcase your products or services. Be sure to include high-quality images and detailed descriptions to attract potential customers. Another digital tool to consider is social media. Platforms such as Instagram and Facebook can be excellent marketing channels to reach a larger audience. Utilize these platforms to connect with potential customers and build a community around your brand. Consider using e-commerce platforms such as Etsy or Amazon to sell your products. These platforms provide a ready-made marketplace and can help you reach customers who are specifically searching for your type of products or services. By harnessing the power of digital tools, you can increase your visibility and reach a wider audience. Monetizing your hobbies is not without its challenges. It requires dedication, hard work and a willingness to continuously learn and adapt. The rewards can be immense. Not only will you have the opportunity to do what you love, but you can also create a sustainable income stream. By identifying opportunities, creating a business plan and utilizing digital tools, you can turn your hobbies into a source of income. So go ahead, unleash your creativity and start monetizing your passions today. You never know where this journey might take you.

III. CREATING A BUSINESS PLAN

Creating a business plan is a crucial step in the process of turning hobbies into a source of income. A business plan acts as a roadmap for the future of an entrepreneurial venture, outlining the goals, strategies and financial projections necessary for success. The first component of a business plan is the executive summary, which provides an overview of the entire plan and highlights its key points. This section should be concise but persuasive, as it serves as a tool to capture the attention of potential investors or partners. Next, the product or service description should be articulated in detail, emphasizing its unique features and benefits. This section allows the reader to understand the value proposition and the target market segment that the venture aims to serve. A market analysis should be conducted to gain a thorough understanding of the industry and competition. This analysis will help the entrepreneur identify market trends, potential customers and any barriers to entry that may exist. A marketing and sales strategy must be developed to effectively promote the product or service and reach the target market. This strategy may involve methods such as social media marketing, influencer collaborations or traditional advertising channels, depending on the nature of the venture. A comprehensive financial plan is also essential, consisting of income statements, balance sheets and cash flow projections. This will enable the entrepreneur to assess the financial viability of the business and make informed decisions. It is important to consider the funding requirements and potential sources of capital that may be necessary to launch and scale the venture. This could include personal savings, loans from financial institutions or partnerships with investors. A risk assessment should be conducted to identify potential challenges and develop contingency plans. This analysis will help the entrepreneur mitigate risk and ensure the long-term sustainability of the business.

Digital tools have revolutionized the process of creating a business plan, making it more accessible and efficient for aspiring entrepreneurs. Online platforms and software applications provide templates and frameworks that guide individuals through each step of the planning process. These tools allow entrepreneurs to input their product or service information, market research, financial projections, another relevant data, generating a professionally formatted business plan document. The use of such tools simplifies the task of creating a business plan, particularly for individuals who may not have prior experience or knowledge in this area. Digital platforms offer collaboration features that facilitate teamwork and feedback from mentors or advisors, enabling aspiring entrepreneurs to refine their ideas and optimize their plans. The accessibility of these tools further democratizes entrepreneurship, allowing anyone with a passion and ambition to transform their hobbies into a profitable business venture. Creating a business plan is an essential step in turning hobbies into a source of income. A well-developed business plan serves as a roadmap for success and provides a thorough analysis of the venture's market potential, financial feasibility and growth strategies. Digital tools have made the process of creating a business plan more accessible and efficient, enabling aspiring entrepreneurs to leverage templates and frameworks to generate professional documents. These tools also facilitate collaboration and feedback, allowing individuals to re-fine their ideas and optimize their plans. By following the steps outlined in a business plan, individuals can confidently monetize their passion and turn their hobbies into a sustainable source of income. With determination, creativity and a sound business plan, individuals can combine their love for what they do with financial success.

DEFINING THE OVERALL BUSINESS CONCEPT AND GOALS

Defining the overall business concept and goals is a critical step in transforming a hobby into a viable source of income. The business concept is the core idea that drives the entire endeavor, providing a clear direction for the business. It involves identifying the specific hobby or passion that will be monetized and understanding how it can be translated into a product or service that meets a market need. To begin, it is important to thoroughly evaluate the chosen hobby to determine its feasibility as a business concept. This involves considering factors such as market demand, competition and scalability. While it may be tempting to get carried away by the excitement of turning a passion into profit, it is crucial to approach this step with a level-headed mindset, objectively assessing whether the hobby can be converted into a sustainable business. Once the feasibility has been confirmed, the next step is to define the goals of the business. These goals provide a roadmap for success and help the entrepreneur stay focused on their vision. It is important to set both short-term and long-term goals that are specific, measurable, achievable, relevant and time-bound (SMART goals). For example, a short-term goal may be to launch the business within six months, while a long-term goal could involve achieving a certain level of annual revenue within three years. In addition to setting goals, it is critical to develop a solid business plan that outlines the strategy and tactics to achieve those goals. This plan acts as a blueprint for the business, providing a detailed roadmap for how the entrepreneur will monetize their hobby. The business plan should include components such as market analysis, target audience identification, competitive analysis, marketing and sales strategies, financial projections and operational plans.

Market analysis is an essential part of the business plan, as it helps the entrepreneur gain insights into the target market's needs and preferences. This analysis involves conducting thorough research on market trends, customer demographics, competitors and potential opportunities and threats. By understanding the market landscape, the entrepreneur can tailor their product or service to meet the specific needs of their target audience, increasing the chances of success. Identifying the target audience is another crucial aspect of the business plan, as it helps to focus marketing efforts and tailor the product or service to meet the needs of the intended customers. Understanding the target audience's demographics, interests and preferences enables the entrepreneur to craft effective marketing messages and strategies that resonate with them. Competitive analysis is equally important as it helps the entrepreneur identify their direct and indirect competitors and gain insights into their strengths, weaknesses and strategies. This analysis enables the entrepreneur to position their product or service in a way that differentiates it from the competition and offers a unique value proposition to customers. The marketing and sales strategies outlined in the business plan provide a roadmap for how the entrepreneur will attract customers and generate revenue. This may include digital marketing techniques such as social media advertising, content marketing, search engine optimization and email marketing. By leveraging these digital tools effectively, the entrepreneur can reach a wider audience and generate leads that convert into customers. Financial projections are another critical component of the business plan, as they provide an estimate of the revenue, expenses and profitability of the business over a specific period. These projections help the entrepreneur understand the financial viability of their business concept and make informed decisions about pricing, cost management and revenue generation.

Operational plans detail the day-to-day operations required to run the business smoothly. This includes aspects such as production, inventory management, customer service and fulfillment. By clearly defining these operational processes, the entrepreneur can ensure efficient and effective execution of their business concept. Defining the overall business concept and goals is a crucial step in monetizing a hobby and turning it into a source of income. This involves evaluating the feasibility of the hobby as a business concept, setting SMART goals and developing a comprehensive business plan. By undertaking these steps, the entrepreneur can lay a strong foundation for transforming their passion into a profitable venture.

DETERMINING THE MAIN OBJECTIVE OF MONETIZING THE HOBBY

Determining the main objective of monetizing a hobby is a crucial step in the process of turning one's passion into a source of income. It is essential to have a clear vision and purpose behind the decision to monetize a hobby, as it can significantly impact the success and sustainability of the venture. The primary objective of monetizing a hobby can vary depending on the individual's goals and aspirations. For some, the main objective may be financial independence and self-sufficiency, while others may seek to enhance their existing career or explore new opportunities within their chosen field. Regardless of the specific objective, the process of monetization requires careful consideration and planning to ensure that it aligns with one's personal and professional goals. One of the main objectives of monetizing a hobby is achieving financial independence and self-sufficiency. Many individuals are drawn to the idea of making money from their hobbies as a means of breaking free from the constraints of a traditional nine-to-five job. By turning their passion into a source of income, they can enjoy greater flexibility and control over their time and resources. Monetizing a hobby can provide a pathway to financial security and stability, allowing individuals to pursue their passions while still meeting their financial obligations. Earning a consistent income from a hobby can empower individuals to focus more on their creative pursuits and invest time and resources into further developing their skills and expertise.

Another objective of monetizing a hobby is to enhance one's

existing career or professional development. Many individuals find that their hobbies complement their professional aspirations and can be leveraged to gain a competitive edge in their chosen field. For example, a graphic designer may monetize their passion for illustration by offering freelance services or selling their artwork online. By incorporating their hobby into their professional portfolio, they can demonstrate their creativity and versatility to potential clients and employers. Monetizing a hobby in this context not only opens up additional income streams but also enables individuals to diversify their skillset and gain real-world experience in their field of interest. Monetizing a hobby can serve as an opportunity for individuals to explore new possibilities and embark on a career transition. Many people find themselves dissatisfied or unfulfilled in their current careers and yearn for something more meaningful and personally rewarding. By turning their hobby into a source of income, they can bridge the gap between their passion and their career and create a pathway to a more fulfilling professional life. This objective of monetization allows individuals to pursue their dreams and aspirations, even if it means starting from scratch or taking a leap of faith. It encourages individuals to embrace their true passion and overcome the fear of failure, opening doors to endless possibilities and the potential for personal and professional growth. Determining the main objective of monetizing a hobby is essential to successfully turn one's passion into a source of income. Whether the primary objective is financial independence, professional enhancement or career transition, having a clear vision and purpose behind the decision to monetize a hobby is crucial. It enables individuals to align their efforts and resources to achieve their goals, whether it be achieving financial security and flexibility, enhancing their existing career or exploring new opportunities. Monetizing a hobby allows individuals to pursue their passions and create a more fulfilling professional life, empowering them to embrace their dreams and aspirations. The process of monetization requires careful planning and consideration to ensure that it remains in line with one's personal and professional objectives. By doing so, individuals can unlock the full potential of their passion and embark on a journey of self-discovery and financial success.

SETTING ACHIEVABLE SHORT-TERM AND LONG-TERM GOALS

Setting achievable short-term and long-term goals is essential when it comes to monetizing your passion and turning your hobbies into a source of income. Without clear goals in mind, it can be easy to lose focus and become overwhelmed by the seemingly endless possibilities. By breaking down your aspirations into manageable chunks, you can create a roadmap for success and maintain momentum along the way. In the short-term, it is crucial to establish specific and realistic goals that are attainable within a relatively short timeframe. These short-term goals act as steppingstones towards your ultimate vision of monetizing your passion. For example, if you are an avid photographer looking to make money from your hobby, a short-term goal could be to build an impressive portfolio showcasing your best work. This can be achieved by dedicating time each week to capturing new images, editing them to perfection and organizing them in a professional manner. By setting this goal, you are actively working towards creating a solid foundation for your future endeavors. Another short-term goal could be to identify potential markets or niches that align with your passion. Researching and assessing the demand for products or services related to your hobby is a crucial step towards generating income. For instance, if you are a skilled painter, you may consider exploring the market for commissioned artwork or teaching art classes. By setting a goal to conduct market research and identify potential opportunities, you are positioning yourself to capitalize on existing demand and monetize your skills effectively. Equally important are long-term goals that set the trajectory for your journey towards monetization. Unlike short-term goals, long-term goals may take months or even years to accomplish. These goals keep you motivated and focused on the bigger picture. For example, if you aspire to become a full-time freelance writer, a long-term goal could be to secure a steady stream of clients who regularly seek your services. This goal necessitates consistent effort in marketing your skills, networking with potential clients and delivering high-quality work. By setting this long-term goal, you are establishing a roadmap for achieving financial independence and sustainability in your chosen field. Long-term goals can also involve scaling your monetization efforts and expanding your reach. For instance, if you have been successfully selling handmade jewelry online, a long-term goal could be to open a physical store or collaborate with retailers to stock your products. This goal requires strategic planning, financial preparation and establishing a solid reputation within the industry. By setting this goal, you are aspiring to take your passion to new heights and reach a wider audience. In order to effectively set achievable goals, it is crucial to consider the SMART criteria: specific, measurable, achievable, relevant and time-bound. Each goal should be clearly defined, measurable in terms of progress and success, realistic given your circumstances, relevant to your ultimate vision and have a timeline for completion. By adhering to the SMART criteria, you are ensuring that your goals are not only achievable but also aligned with your long-term aspirations.

Setting achievable short-term and long-term goals is instrumental in successfully monetizing your passion and turning your hobbies into a source of income. These goals provide direction, purpose and a framework for your entrepreneurial journey. By breaking down your vision into manageable chunks, conducting research and adhering to the SMART criteria, you can effectively navigate the path towards financial independence while doing what you love. Remember, setting goals is just the beginning; the real work lies in taking consistent action towards achieving them. With determination, perseverance and a clear roadmap, you can transform your passions into a profitable endeavor.

CONDUCTING MARKET RESEARCH AND FEASIBILITY ANALYSIS

Conducting market research and feasibility analysis is a crucial step when looking to monetize your hobbies and turn them into a source of income. Market research helps you gain a deep understanding of your target audience, their preferences and their needs. By conducting market research, you can identify the demand for your hobby and assess if there is a viable market for your product or service. To conduct market research effectively, you need to employ various methodologies. One common approach is to conduct surveys and questionnaires to gather insights from potential customers. These surveys can ask questions regarding their interests, preferences and willingness to pay for products or services related to your hobby. By gathering this data, you can assess if there is a sufficient market size to support your venture and what price points customers are willing to pay. Another effective market research method is to analyze your competitors and their offerings. By studying your competitors, you can identify any gaps or opportunities in the market that you can exploit. This analysis helps you understand how you can differentiate yourself and add value to your potential customers. For example, if you are passionate about photography and want to start a photography business, you can analyze the local photography market to see if there are already established businesses and what services they offer. By identifying any gaps in the market, such as a lack of affordable portrait photography services, you can position yourself to cater to that specific segment. A feasibility analysis is another crucial step in turning your hobbies into a source of income. Feasibility analysis involves evaluating the practicality and viability of your business idea. This assessment helps you determine if your hobby can be transformed into a profitable venture and if it aligns with your personal and financial goals. One aspect of feasibility analysis is assessing the financial viability of your hobby-turned-business. This entails conducting a thorough financial analysis to determine the costs involved in starting and running your business. These costs can include equipment, supplies, marketing and overhead expenses. By quantifying these costs, you can estimate the revenue needed to cover expenses and generate a profit.

A feasibility analysis examines the resources and skills required to transform your hobby into a business. This assessment helps you determine if you possess the necessary expertise or if you need to acquire additional knowledge or skills. For instance, if your hobby is baking and you want to start a bakery, you may need to enhance your culinary skills or hire experienced bakers. Identifying any resource or skill gaps early on allows you to plan and prepare accordingly. In addition to market research and feasibility analysis, digital tools can play a significant role in monetizing your passion. The internet and social media platforms have revolutionized the way businesses reach and engage with customers. Utilizing digital tools, such as social media marketing, search engine optimization (SEO) and e-commerce platforms, can help you effectively promote your products or services, reach a broader audience and generate sales.

For example, if you are interested in handcrafted jewelry and want to sell your creations, you can leverage social media platforms like Instagram or Facebook to showcase your products and connect with potential customers. By strategically using hashtags, engaging with followers and collaborating with influencers, you can increase your visibility and attract customers to your online store or website. Conducting market research and feasibility analysis are fundamental in the process of monetizing your hobbies and turning them into a source of income. Through market research, you can identify the demand for your product or service and assess the viability of your venture. Feasibility analysis, on the other hand, helps you evaluate the financial and practical aspects of your business idea. Utilizing digital tools can enhance your ability to reach a wider audience and generate sales. By carefully considering these factors, you can successfully transform your passion into a profitable venture.

ANALYZING THE MARKET POTENTIAL AND COMPETITION IN THE CHOSEN NICHE

Analyzing the market potential and competition in the chosen niche is a crucial step in the process of turning hobbies into a source of income. Before diving headfirst into a business venture, it is essential to understand the market dynamics and identify the potential customers for your product or service.

Conducting a thorough market analysis will provide valuable insights into the demand for your offering and the competition you may face. One of the first steps in analyzing the market potential is identifying the target audience for your product or service. This involves understanding who your potential customers are, what their needs and preferences are and how your offering can fulfill those needs better than the existing alternatives in the market.

For example, if your chosen niche is woodworking, you need to determine whether your target market comprises professional craftsmen, DIY enthusiasts or both. Understanding your target audience will help tailor your offering to their specific needs and preferences, giving you a competitive edge in the market.

Once you have identified your target audience, it is essential to assess the market demand for your product or service. This involves analyzing the size of the market, the growth rate and any trends that may impact the demand for your offering. For example, if you are planning to monetize your passion for organic gardening, you might want to research the size of the organic food market, the consumer trends towards healthy eating and any government policies or regulations supporting organic farming. This analysis will help you determine if there is a viable market for your offering and whether the demand is likely to increase or decrease in the future. Alongside market demand, it is crucial to analyze the competition in your chosen niche. Identifying your direct and indirect competitors will help you understand their strengths, weaknesses and market positioning. Direct competitors are those who offer similar products or services to the same target audience, while indirect competitors may provide alternative solutions to fulfill the same customer needs. For example, if you are planning to start a photography business, your direct competitors may include other professional photographers in your area, while your indirect competitors may include stock photography websites or smartphone apps that offer photo editing tools. By studying your competition, you can gain insights into their pricing strategies, marketing tactics and customer satisfaction levels, enabling you to differentiate yourself and create a unique value proposition. In addition to understanding your competition, it is crucial to assess the barriers to entry in your chosen niche. These barriers may include legal requirements, certifications or significant capital investment.

For example, if you plan to start a catering business, you may need to comply with health and safety regulations, obtain permits and invest in a commercial kitchen. By understanding the barriers to entry, you can evaluate whether you have the resources and capabilities to overcome these challenges and establish a sustainable business in your chosen niche.

Conducting a SWOT analysis (Strengths, Weaknesses, Opportunities and Threats) can provide a comprehensive understanding of the market potential and competition in your chosen niche. This analysis allows you to assess your own strengths and weaknesses, as well as the opportunities and threats that exist in the market. By identifying your strengths, such as unique skills or expertise, you can leverage them to gain a competitive advantage. Likewise, by acknowledging your weaknesses, you can work on improving them or seek partnerships to fill the gaps in your offering. Identifying opportunities and threats will help you anticipate market trends, adapt your offering accordingly and mitigate any potential risks. Analyzing the market potential and competition in the chosen niche is a critical step in monetizing your passion and turning your hobbies into a source of income. By understanding your target audience, assessing market demand and analyzing the competition, you can create a compelling value proposition and position yourself for success. Identifying the barriers to entry and conducting a SWOT analysis will help you evaluate the feasibility and sustainability of your business venture. Armed with this knowledge, you can confidently launch your business and embark on a journey to do what you love while making a sustainable income.

ASSESSING THE FINANCIAL VIABILITY AND SUSTAINABILITY OF THE BUSINESS

Assessing the financial viability and sustainability of a business is a crucial step in turning your hobbies into a source of income. While it may be tempting to jump headfirst into monetizing your passion, it is essential to take a step back and objectively evaluate whether your hobby can generate enough income to sustain a business in the long run. There are several factors to consider when assessing the financial viability of your venture.

First and foremost, you need to determine the market demand for your product or service. Is there a target audience that is willing to pay for what you have to offer? Conducting market research and gathering data on consumer behavior can provide valuable insights into the demand for your hobby-based business. By understanding the needs and preferences of potential customers, you can tailor your offerings to ensure that there is a viable market for your products or services. Assessing the competitive landscape is crucial in determining the financial sustainability of your business. Are there already established businesses in your industry? If so, what sets your business apart from the competition? Conducting a thorough analysis of your competitors can help you identify gaps in the market that you can fill with your unique offerings. Understanding the pricing strategies and business models of your competitors can guide you in setting competitive prices for your products or services. Another aspect to consider when assessing the financial viability of your hobby-based business is the cost structure and profitability. You need to evaluate the costs involved in running your business and whether the revenue generated will be able to cover those expenses. Consider the cost of raw materials, production, marketing and overhead costs such as rent and utilities. It is essential to carefully estimate your expenses and ensure that your pricing strategy allows for a profitable margin. Achieving financial sustainability requires careful financial planning and forecasting. It is crucial to create a realistic financial plan that takes into account factors such as sales projections, cash flow and break-even analysis. By projecting your revenue and expenses over a specific period, you can gain insights into the financial viability and sustainability of your business. This can also help you identify potential financial risks and create contingency plans to mitigate them. Understanding the financial metrics that are relevant to your industry can help you assess the viability of your business. Key performance indicators such as gross margin, net profit margin and return on investment can provide insights into the financial health of your business. Comparing your financial metrics with industry benchmarks can give you a better understanding of where your business stands and identify areas for improvement. Incorporating digital tools and technology can significantly contribute to the financial viability and sustainability of your business. Digital platforms, such as e-commerce websites and social media platforms, can help you reach a broader audience and increase sales. Leveraging digital marketing strategies, such as search engine optimization and social media advertising, can effectively promote your products or services and drive traffic to your online store. Assessing the financial viability and sustainability of your hobby-based business is vital to ensure its long-term success. By thoroughly evaluating market demand, understanding the competitive landscape and considering the cost structure and profitability, you can make informed decisions about monetizing your passion. Financial planning and forecasting, along with the use of digital tools, can further enhance the likelihood of achieving financial sustainability. Remember that while turning your hobbies into income is an exciting endeavor, it requires careful analysis and strategic decision-making. With the right approach, you can do what you love and make money from it.

DEVELOPING A MARKETING AND SALES STRATEGY

Developing a marketing and sales strategy is a crucial step in monetizing one's passion and turning hobbies into a source of income. Once the business plan has been created and the opportunities have been identified, it is important to devise a strategy that effectively promotes and sells the products or services being offered. A key aspect of this strategy is understanding the target market and how to reach them through various marketing channels. One of the first steps in developing a marketing and sales strategy is conducting market research to gain a better understanding of the target audience. This research involves gathering information about the potential customers, their preferences and their purchase behavior. By understanding the needs and desires of the target market, individuals can tailor their marketing messages and sales techniques to effectively attract and retain customers. This research can be done through surveys, interviews or by using digital tools that provide insights into consumer data and trends. Once the target market has been identified, it is important to choose the right marketing channels to reach them. Digital tools and platforms offer a range of options for promoting products or services, such as social media marketing, content marketing, email marketing, search engine optimization (SEO) and paid advertising. Each of these channels has its own advantages and disadvantages and it is important to assess which ones are most suitable for reaching the target market. Social media marketing is a powerful tool for monetizing one's passion as it allows individuals to reach a wide audience and engage with potential customers. Platforms such as Facebook, Instagram and Twitter provide opportunities to showcase products or services, build brand awareness and interact with customers through comments and direct messages. Content marketing, on the other hand, involves creating and sharing valuable content that is relevant to the target market. This could be in the form of blog posts, videos or podcasts that offer insights, tips or advice related to the hobby or passion being monetized. By providing valuable content, individuals can position themselves as experts in their field and build trust with potential customers. Email marketing is another effective channel for promoting products or services. By building an email list of potential customers, individuals can send targeted messages and offers directly to their inbox. This allows for personalization and customization of marketing messages, increasing the chances of conversions and sales. Search engine optimization (SEO) is also important for ensuring that potential customers can find the website or online store when searching for related products or services. By optimizing the website's content, meta tags and keywords, individuals can improve their search engine rankings and attract more organic traffic. Paid advertising also plays a role in the marketing and sales strategy. Platforms such as Google Ads and Facebook Ads allow individuals to target specific demographics, interests and behaviors, ensuring that their ads are seen by the right audience. Paid advertising can be particularly effective for reaching a new audience or boosting sales during specific promotions or campaigns. In addition to marketing channels, the sales strategy should also include elements such as pricing, sales promotions and customer relationship management. Pricing is an important consideration that should be aligned with the target market and value proposition. Sales promotions, such as discounts or limited-time offers, can help generate excitement and urge potential customers to make a purchase. Maintaining strong customer relationships is critical for repeat business and word-of-mouth referrals. This can be achieved through excellent customer service, personalized interactions and loyalty programs. Developing a marketing and sales strategy is an essential step in monetizing one's passion and turning hobbies into a source of income. Through market research and understanding the target market, individuals can tailor their messages and choose the right marketing channels to reach potential customers. Digital tools, such as social media marketing, content marketing, email marketing, SEO and paid advertising, provide effective ways to promote products or services. Pricing, sales promotions and customer relationship management also play key roles in the overall sales strategy. By developing an effective marketing and sales strategy, individuals can successfully monetize their passion and make money from doing what they love.

IDENTIFYING TARGET CUSTOMERS AND OUTLINING EFFECTIVE PROMOTIONAL TECHNIQUES

Identifying target customers and outlining effective promotional techniques are crucial steps in monetizing your hobbies and turning them into a source of income. Understanding who your target customers are is essential for crafting effective marketing strategies and reaching the right audience. By identifying your target customers, you can tailor your promotional techniques to their specific needs and preferences, increasing the chances of success in monetizing your passion. To identify your target customers, it is important to conduct thorough market research. By analyzing the market trends and consumer behavior, you can gain insights into who your potential customers are and what they are looking for. This research can include demographic data, such as age, gender and location, as well as psychographic information, such as interests, values and lifestyle choices. By understanding your target customers on a deeper level, you can create a more targeted approach to promoting your products or services, increasing the likelihood of attracting those who are genuinely interested in your hobby. Once you have identified your target customers, you can outline effective promotional techniques to reach them. In today's digital age, utilizing online platforms and digital tools is essential for effective promotion. Social media platforms provide a cost-effective way to reach a wide audience and engage with potential customers. Creating engaging and visually appealing content, such as videos, images and blog posts, can help generate interest and increase exposure for your hobby-based business. Utilizing hashtags and targeted advertisements can further enhance your online presence and reach the right audience. In addition to online promotion, utilizing offline promotional techniques can also be effective in reaching your target customers. Networking events, trade shows and community gatherings provide opportunities to showcase your products or services directly to potential customers. By participating in these events, you can connect with individuals who share a similar interest and are more likely to be interested in what you have to offer. Offering free samples or demonstrations can help create a positive and lasting impression, increasing the likelihood of future sales. Collaborating with influencers or industry experts can also be beneficial in promoting your hobby-based business. Influencers often have a large and engaged following, making them ideal partners for reaching your target customers. By partnering with influencers who align with your brand and values, you can leverage their reach and credibility to increase brand awareness and attract new customers. Collaborating with industry experts can also help establish your credibility and expertise, further enhancing your promotional efforts.

In order to ensure the effectiveness of your promotional techniques, it is important to continuously track and analyze the results of your marketing strategies. This can be done through various analytics tools available online, such as Google Analytics and social media insights. By monitoring the performance of your promotional campaigns, you can identify what works and what doesn't, allowing you to make informed decisions and refine your strategies accordingly. This data-driven approach can help optimize your promotional efforts and maximize your return on investment. Identifying target customers and outlining effective promotional techniques are crucial steps in monetizing your hobbies and turning them into a source of income. By understanding who your target customers are and tailoring your promotional techniques to their needs and preferences, you can increase the chances of success in attracting genuine interest and generating sales. Utilizing online and offline promotional techniques, collaborating with influencers and industry experts and continuously monitoring and analyzing the results of your marketing strategies can help you effectively promote your hobby-based business and achieve financial success. So, with the right strategies and determination, you can do what you love and make money from it.

CREATING A PRICING STRUCTURE AND SALES MODEL SUITABLE FOR THE HOBBY-BASED BUSINESS

Creating a pricing structure and sales model suitable for a hobby-based business is crucial to ensure profitability and sustainability. When transitioning a hobby into a business, it is essential to carefully assess the market, identify competitors and determine the unique value proposition of the product or service. This will lay the foundation for setting appropriate prices that reflect the perceived value while remaining competitive. Conducting market research, including surveys and focus groups, can provide insights into customers' willingness to pay and their expectations regarding pricing. It is important to consider the costs associated with producing and delivering the product or service. This includes direct costs like materials, equipment and labor, as well as indirect costs such as marketing and overhead expenses. By carefully analyzing these factors, a pricing structure can be established that covers costs, generates profit and appeals to the target market. The choice of sales model is also integral to the success of a hobby-based business. Several options can be considered, depending on the nature of the hobby and the target audience. One popular sales model for hobby-based businesses is direct sales, which involves selling products or services directly to customers through outlets such as craft fairs, farmers markets or online platforms. This model allows for personal interaction with customers, enabling the seller to showcase their passion and expertise, answer any questions and cultivate loyal relationships. Another sales model worth considering is online sales, utilizing e-commerce platforms and social media channels. With the growing popularity of online shopping, this model offers a convenient and accessible way to reach a broader customer base. It also provides opportunities for customization, allowing hobbyists to showcase their unique creations and connect with like-minded individuals globally. Whichever sales model is chosen, leveraging digital tools is essential to maximize monetization opportunities. Digital tools can assist in various aspects of the business, from customer acquisition to sales and marketing. For instance, social media platforms like Facebook, Instagram and Pinterest can be utilized to showcase products or services, engage with customers and build brand loyalty. By regularly posting high-quality photos or videos and sharing informative content, hobbyists can create a brand identity and attract potential customers. These platforms often offer features that facilitate direct selling, such as shoppable posts or integrated shopping carts, streamlining the purchasing process for customers. Email marketing tools can be utilized to send personalized newsletters and promotions to be existing customers, encouraging repeat purchases and word-of-mouth referrals.

In addition to social media and email marketing, search engine optimization (SEO) techniques can play a significant role in driving traffic to a hobby-based business's website or online store. By optimizing website content, meta tags and keywords, hobbyists can improve their organic search rankings on search engine results pages. This increases the visibility of the business and enhances the chances of attracting potential customers. Paid advertising through platforms like Google Ads or Facebook Ads can be employed to target specific demographics or geographic locations, further increasing the visibility and reach of the business. These digital tools provide hobbyists with cost-effective and efficient methods to promote their products or services and generate sales. Creating a pricing structure and sales model suitable for a hobby-based business requires careful consideration and analysis. By conducting market research and assessing costs, hobbyists can establish a pricing structure that reflects the perceived value of their products or services while remaining competitive. Choosing an appropriate sales model, whether direct sales or online sales, allows hobbyists to connect with customers and expand their reach. Leveraging digital tools such as social media, email marketing and SEO techniques enhances the monetization opportunities for hobby-based businesses. With the right pricing structure, sales model and digital tools, individuals can successfully turn their hobbies into a profitable source of income. Turning your hobbies into a source of income can be an exciting and fulfilling way to pursue your passion while also making money. It allows you to do what you love and potentially create a successful business out of it. Monetizing your hobbies requires careful planning and the use of digital tools to maximize your chances of success. By learning how to identify opportunities, create a business plan and effectively utilize digital tools, you can transform your hobbies into a viable source of income. The first step in monetizing your hobbies is to identify opportunities that align with your interests. Consider the skills you have developed through your hobbies and how they can be applied in a business context. For example, if you are an avid photographer, you can start a photography business or sell your photos online. If you have a passion for cooking, you could start a catering service or create an online cooking course. By thinking creatively, you can find unique ways to turn your hobbies into income-generating ventures.

Once you have identified opportunities, the next step is to create a business plan. A business plan is essential for outlining your goals, strategies and financial projections. It helps you understand the market, identify your target audience and develop a competitive edge. Your business plan should include a description of your products or services, a market analysis, a marketing strategy and a financial plan. It should also outline your short-term and long-term goals and provide a roadmap for achieving them. By creating a well-thought-out business plan, you increase your chances of success and attract potential investors or partners. In today's digital age, leveraging digital tools is crucial for monetizing your hobbies effectively. The internet provides vast opportunities to promote and sell your products or services. First, you should establish a strong online presence through social media platforms and a professional website. Social media allows you to connect with your target audience and showcase your work. It also helps you build a community of loyal followers who can potentially become customers. A professional website is essential for showcasing your portfolio or products, providing information about your business and facilitating online sales.

In addition to social media and a website, there are various digital tools that can help you monetize your hobbies. For example, if you are a creative artist, platforms like Etsy or Shopify can provide a platform for selling your handmade crafts or artwork. If you are a writer, platforms like Medium or self-publishing platforms like Amazon Kindle Direct Publishing allow you to share and sell your written work. Online learning platforms like Udemy or Skillshare enable you to create and sell online courses based on your expertise. By leveraging these digital tools, you can reach a wider audience and increase your chances of generating income from your hobbies. Turning your hobbies into a source of income is an exciting and rewarding endeavor. By identifying opportunities that align with your interests, creating a well-thought-out business plan and effectively leveraging digital tools, you can monetize your hobbies and do what you love while making money. It is essential to think creatively and explore unique ways to turn your hobbies into income-generating ventures. With the right mindset and strategic planning, you can transform your hobbies into a successful business and achieve financial independence while pursuing your true passion.

IV. LEVERAGING DIGITAL TOOLS FOR MONETIZATION

In today's digital age, the possibilities for monetizing your passion have never been greater. With the power of the internet and a myriad of digital tools at your disposal, turning your hobbies into a source of income is easier than ever before. From online platforms that connect you with potential customers and clients to social media channels that help you build a strong personal brand, digital tools can be incredibly useful in your quest to monetize your passion. One of the most effective digital tools for monetization is the use of online marketplaces. These platforms provide a convenient way to sell your products or services to a wide audience and reach customers who may be interested in what you have to offer. Whether you're a talented artist looking to sell your paintings or a skilled writer offering freelance writing services, online marketplaces like Etsy and Fiverr can connect you with potential buyers from all around the world. These platforms not only give you access to a global market, but they also provide tools and features that can help you streamline your business operations, such as secure payment processing and automatic order fulfillment. In addition to online marketplaces, social media channels have also proven to be highly effective in monetizing hobbies. Platforms like Instagram, YouTube and TikTok offer a space for individuals to showcase their talents and build a loyal following. By consistently creating and sharing content that resonates with your target audience, you can attract a large number of followers who are interested in your work. These followers can then be monetized through various means, such as sponsored posts, brand partnerships or even selling your own products or services. The key to success on social media is to provide value to your audience and establish yourself as an authority in your niche. This will not only help you attract more followers but also create trust and credibility, which are essential for monetizing your passion. Another digital tool that can be leveraged for monetization is personal branding. In today's highly connected world, your personal brand is more important than ever before. Building a strong personal brand allows you to differentiate yourself from competitors and establish a unique identity that resonates with your target audience. By utilizing digital tools such as websites, blogs and social media platforms, you can create a brand image that showcases your expertise, values and personality. This branding can then be used to attract opportunities for monetization, such as speaking engagements, collaborations or even endorsement deals. Investing time and effort into building a strong personal brand is crucial for effectively monetizing your passion. Digital tools can also be used to optimize your monetization strategies. Through the use of analytics and tracking tools, you can gain valuable insights into your target audience's preferences, behaviors and demographics. This data can then be used to refine your marketing efforts and tailor your products or services to meet the specific needs of your customers. Digital tools can also help you automate processes, such as customer communication or inventory management, allowing you to focus on the creative aspects of your passion while still running a successful business. Leveraging digital tools is essential for monetizing your passion in today's digital age. From online marketplaces that connect you with potential customers to social media platforms that help you build a strong personal brand, these tools offer countless opportunities to turn your hobbies into a source of income. By utilizing these digital tools effectively, you can reach a wider audience, build a loyal following and optimize your monetization strategies. So, if you're ready to do what you love and make money from it, embracing the power of digital tools is the key to success.

ESTABLISHING AN ONLINE PRESENCE

Establishing an online presence is crucial for individuals looking to monetize their hobbies and turn them into a source of income. With the rapid growth of the internet and the increasing reliance on digital tools, having a strong online presence is essential for reaching a wider audience and capturing potential customers. One of the first steps in establishing an online presence is creating a website or a blog dedicated to showcasing one's hobbies and the products or services associated with them. This website serves as the online storefront, where visitors can learn more about the hobbyist's offerings, make purchases and engage with the content. It is important to have a clean and user-friendly design, with clear navigation and intuitive interfaces to make the browsing experience enjoyable and hassle-free for potential customers. Ensuring that the website is mobile-friendly is essential, as an increasing number of people access the internet using their smartphones. A mobile-responsive design will allow the website to adapt to different screen sizes and maintain functionality, giving all users a seamless experience regardless of the device they use. In addition to a website, social media platforms play a vital role in establishing an online presence. Social media allows hobbyists to connect with their target audience on a more personal level, engage in conversations and share updates about their offerings. By carefully selecting the appropriate social media platforms that align with their target audience and objectives, hobbyists can expand their reach and attract potential customers. For instance, a photographer looking to monetize his passion could benefit from using platforms like Instagram or Pinterest, where visual content is highly valued, while a fitness enthusiast could target platforms like Facebook or YouTube to share workout videos and fitness tips. Engaging consistently with the audience is crucial for building a strong online presence. Hobbyists should regularly update their website or blog with fresh content, be it informative articles, product showcases or tutorials. This not only keeps the audience interested and engaged but also helps with search engine optimization (SEO), improving the visibility of the website on search engine result pages and driving organic traffic. Interacting with the audience through social media platforms, responding to comments and messages promptly and addressing any concerns or inquiries help establish credibility, trust and customer loyalty. Another effective way to establish an online presence is by leveraging digital marketing strategies. Pay-per-click (PPC) advertising, search engine marketing (SEM) and search engine optimization (SEO) are some of the commonly used strategies to increase visibility and drive targeted traffic to a website or blog. PPC advertising allows hobbyists to display ads on search engine result pages or other websites, paying only when a user clicks on the ad. SEM involves optimizing the website's visibility on search engines through paid advertisements and organic search results. SEO, on the other hand, involves optimizing the website's content, structure and backlink profile to improve its ranking on search engine result pages, resulting in increased organic traffic. Email marketing is another effective digital tool to establish an online presence. By building an email list of interested prospects and customers, hobbyists can send regular newsletters, promotional offers or updates, keeping them engaged and increasing brand recall. It is important to ensure that the emails are relevant, personalized and provide value to the recipients. Hobbyists should be mindful of spam laws and respect the privacy of their subscribers by providing the option to unsubscribe from the mailing list.

Establishing an online presence is crucial for individuals looking to monetize their hobbies and turn them into a source of income. By creating a website or blog, leveraging social media platforms, engaging consistently with the audience and implementing digital marketing strategies, hobbyists can reach a wider audience, increase visibility and drive traffic to their offerings. The digital landscape offers abundant opportunities for individuals to do what they love and make money from it and establishing a strong online presence is the first step towards realizing those opportunities.

BUILDING A WEBSITE OR BLOG TO SHOWCASE PRODUCTS OR SERVICES

Building a website or blog to showcase products or services is a crucial step in the process of monetizing your passion. In today's digital age, having an online presence is essential for any business or individual looking to reach a wider audience and generate income. Creating a website or blog allows you to showcase your products or services in a visually appealing and informative manner, making it easier for potential customers or clients to learn about what you have to offer. This platform also enables you to establish your brand identity and build credibility in your chosen industry. One of the key benefits of building a website or blog is the ability to showcase your products or services in a way that highlights their unique features and benefits. Through the use of high-quality images, detailed descriptions and engaging content, you can effectively communicate the value of what you offer to your target audience. Whether you are selling handmade crafts, offering consulting services or providing digital products, a website or blog provides you with a centralized platform where you can effectively market your offerings to potential customers. A website or blog allows you to establish your brand identity. By creating a visually cohesive and user-friendly platform, you can convey your unique style, values and mission to your audience. This not only helps you stand out in a crowded marketplace but also allows potential customers to develop a connection with your brand and develop loyalty. Your website or blog can serve as a representation of your brand's personality and values, helping to differentiate your offerings from competitors and attract your target audience. Building a website or blog can go a long way in building credibility in your chosen industry. In today's digital landscape, consumers often turn to the internet to research and validate the credibility of businesses or individuals before making a purchase or seeking services. Having a well-designed and informative website or blog can help establish trust and confidence in potential customers, as it demonstrates your expertise and commitment to delivering quality products or services. By providing valuable content, testimonials and a transparent overview of your offerings, you can position yourself as a trusted authority in your field and differentiate yourself from competitors. In addition to showcasing your offerings and establishing credibility, a website or blog also enables you to easily reach a wider audience. Unlike traditional brick-and-mortar stores or physical marketing materials, an online platform allows you to reach people from all around the world. By utilizing search engine optimization (SEO) techniques and social media marketing, you can increase your website or blog's visibility and attract more organic traffic. This opens up new opportunities for growth and revenue, as you can now tap into markets that were previously inaccessible. Building a website or blog allows you to create a seamless and convenient purchasing experience for your customers. Integrating an e-commerce platform into your website enables potential customers to browse, select and purchase your products or services directly from your platform. This eliminates the need for customers to visit physical stores or go through complex purchasing processes, making it more likely for them to complete a transaction. By providing a simple and secure purchasing process, you can increase sales and customer satisfaction, ultimately leading to increased revenue.

Building a website or blog to showcase products or services is an essential step in monetizing your passion. It provides a platform for you to effectively market your offerings, establish your brand identity, build credibility, reach a wider audience and create a seamless purchasing experience for your customers. In today's digital age, having an online presence is no longer optional but necessary for individuals and businesses looking to succeed. So, don't miss out on the opportunities that building a website or blog can bring to your passion-turned-business journey.

UTILIZING SOCIAL MEDIA PLATFORMS TO REACH A WIDER AUDIENCE

Utilizing social media platforms to reach a wider audience is essential when it comes to monetizing one's passion. With the power of social media, individuals can connect with people from all over the world and expand their reach beyond their immediate circle. By leveraging platforms such as Facebook, Instagram, Twitter and YouTube, individuals can effectively promote their hobbies and turn them into a source of income. One of the main advantages of utilizing social media platforms is the ability to connect with a vast audience that otherwise would not be accessible through traditional means. With billions of users on platforms such as Facebook and Instagram, individuals have the opportunity to reach potential customers on a global scale. By creating captivating content that showcases their skills and passion, individuals can attract a wide range of individuals who share similar interests. For example, someone who is passionate about photography can create an Instagram account dedicated to sharing their work and tips. By using popular photography hashtags and engaging with other photographers, they can organically grow their following and attract potential clients or sponsors. Using social media platforms allows individuals to establish their personal brand and showcase their expertise. By consistently posting high-quality content and providing value to their audience, individuals can position themselves as experts in their field. This can open doors to various income-generating opportunities such as sponsored posts, collaborations with brands and even speaking engagements or workshops. Through social media platforms, individuals can establish themselves as thought leaders, which can be highly valuable in today's digital landscape. Social media platforms provide a direct line of communication between individuals and their audience. This allows for real-time feedback and engagement, which can be invaluable when it comes to understanding one's target market and tailoring their offerings accordingly. By actively listening to their audience through the comments, direct messages and surveys, individuals can gain valuable insights into what their audience wants and needs. This information can be used to refine their products or services and create offerings that resonate with their target market. For example, a fitness enthusiast who creates workout videos on YouTube can ask their audience for input on what types of routines they would like to see or what challenges they are facing in their fitness journey. This feedback can be used to create targeted content or even develop a fitness program that is specifically tailored to their audience's needs. Social media platforms offer a variety of advertising options that can help individuals reach an even wider audience. By utilizing targeted ads on platforms such as Facebook and Instagram, individuals can ensure that their content is seen by the right people. These platforms provide advanced targeting options that allow individuals to specify the demographics, interests and behaviors of their desired audience. This level of precision ensures that individuals are reaching individuals who are most likely to be interested in their offerings, maximizing the return on their advertising investment. Utilizing social media platforms is crucial when it comes to monetizing one's passion. The ability to reach a wider audience, establish a personal brand, engage with one's audience and utilize targeted advertising are all powerful tools that can help individuals turn their hobbies into a source of income. By harnessing the power of platforms such as Facebook, Instagram, Twitter and YouTube, individuals can connect with like-minded individuals, showcase their skills and attract potential clients or sponsors. Through consistent and valuable content, individuals can establish themselves as experts in their field and position themselves for various income-generating opportunities. By actively listening to their audience, individuals can gain valuable insights and tailor their offerings to meet their audience's needs. Utilizing targeted advertising ensures that individuals are reaching the right people and maximizing their advertising investment. Embracing social media platforms can truly unlock the full potential of turning one's hobbies into a profitable venture.

EXPLORING E-COMMERCE PLATFORMS AND MARKETPLACES

When it comes to monetizing your passion, exploring e-commerce platforms and marketplaces can be a game-changer. These online platforms not only provide a place for you to sell your products and services, but they also offer the opportunity to reach a wider audience and tap into a global market. With the rise of digitalization and the increasing number of people turning to online shopping, e-commerce platforms have become a popular option for entrepreneurs and hobbyists alike.

One of the most well-known e-commerce platforms is Amazon. With its extensive reach and global customer base, Amazon provides an ideal platform for selling a wide range of products. Whether you are creating handmade crafts, writing e-books or selling vintage goods, Amazon offers various options to list, market and sell your products. With their Fulfilled by Amazon (FBA) program, you can even outsource the storage, packaging and shipping of your products, enabling you to focus on creating and expanding your product line. Another popular e-commerce platform is Etsy. Unlike Amazon, Etsy focuses on handmade products, vintage items and craft supplies. If you are passionate about creating unique and one-of-a-kind products, then Etsy might be the perfect platform for you. With its vibrant community of buyers and sellers, Etsy provides a supportive environment for showcasing your creativity and connecting with like-minded individuals. Etsy offers various marketing tools, such as social media integration and coupon codes, to help you promote your products and drive traffic to your store. For those who are looking for a platform to monetize their skills and knowledge, Udemy provides an excellent opportunity. Udemy is an online learning platform that allows individuals to create and sell online courses on various topics. If you have expertise in a particular area, such as photography, cooking or programming, you can create a course and earn money from it. With Udemy's user-friendly interface and extensive reach, you can easily publish your course, set your own prices and attract students from around the world. Udemy provides a range of tools and resources to help you create high-quality courses, including video editing software, course creation guides and marketing tips.

In addition to these popular e-commerce platforms, there are also specialized marketplaces that cater to specific niches. For example, Redbubble is a platform that allows artists and de-signers to sell their artwork in various forms, such as prints, clothing and home decor. If you are passionate about creating art and want to turn it into a source of income, Redbubble pro-vides a platform to showcase your talent and connect with art lovers. Similarly, Turo is a marketplace that enables car owners to rent out their vehicles to travelers. If you have a spare car sitting in your garage, Turo allows you to generate income by sharing it with others. Exploring e-commerce platforms and marketplaces can be a powerful strategy for monetizing your passion. Whether you are creating products, offering services or sharing your knowledge, these platforms offer a range of oppor-tunities to turn your hobbies into income. From global giants like Amazon and Etsy to specialized marketplaces like Redbubble and Turo, there are various platforms available to suit different interests and skills. By leveraging the reach and resources offered by these platforms, you can attract customers, expand your audience and ultimately make money doing what you love. So don't let your hobbies remain a mere pastime - unlock their potential and start monetizing your passion today!

LISTING PRODUCTS OR SERVICES ON ESTABLISHED PLATFORMS LIKE ETSY OR EBAY

Listing products or services on established platforms like Etsy or eBay can be a game-changer for individuals looking to monetize their passion. These platforms provide a ready-made customer base, making it easier to reach a larger audience and increase sales potential. Etsy, for example, is a popular platform for creators and artisans to sell their handmade and vintage items. With over 81 million active buyers, this platform offers a vast marketplace for individuals to showcase their unique creations and tap into a niche market. Etsy provides various tools and resources to help sellers succeed, such as customizable online storefronts, SEO optimization and social media integration. By leveraging these features, sellers can effectively promote their products and attract potential customers. EBay is another established platform that allows individuals to sell a wide range of products. With over 180 million active buyers worldwide, eBay provides sellers with extensive reach and the opportunity to sell to a global market. Whether it's vintage collectibles, electronics or fashion items, eBay offers a versatile platform for sellers to showcase their products. EBay offers seller protection and secure payment options, ensuring a safe and trustworthy experience for both buyers and sellers. This can alleviate any concerns individuals may have when transitioning from a hobbyist to a business owner. Listing products or services on these established platforms provides hobbyists with a platform to showcase their creations, reach a wider customer base and ultimately monetize their passion. By utilizing established platforms like Etsy or eBay, individuals can also benefit from the credibility and trustworthiness associated with these platforms. These platforms have built a strong reputation over time and are trusted by consumers worldwide. When potential customers see products listed on platforms like Etsy or eBay, they are more likely to feel confident about the quality and authenticity of the items. This trust factor can play a significant role in driving sales and attracting customers who may have been hesitant to purchase from unknown sellers. These platforms often have feedback and review systems that allow buyers to leave reviews and ratings for sellers. Positive feedback can serve as a form of social proof and help sellers build credibility and trust with potential customers. This adds an extra layer of validation to the products or services being offered, further enticing customers to make a purchase.

The credibility and trust associated with established platforms like Etsy and eBay can greatly benefit individuals looking to monetize their passion. Listing products or services on established platforms also offers individuals access to valuable data and insights that can inform their business decisions. These platforms provide sellers with analytics and statistics related to their listings, such as the number of views, click-through rates and conversion rates. By analyzing these data points, sellers can gain insights into what products or services are performing well and make informed decisions about pricing, marketing strategies and inventory management. The ability to access such valuable information can help individuals refine their offerings, optimize their listings and ultimately drive more sales. These platforms often offer seller support and educational resources to help sellers navigate the intricacies of online selling, such as tips on

SEO optimization or marketing techniques. By leveraging these resources, individuals can enhance their knowledge and skills in e-commerce, further increasing their chances of success. Listing products or services on established platforms like Etsy or eBay can provide individuals with access to valuable data, insights and support to inform their business decisions and maximize their sales potential. In summary, listing products or services on established platforms like Etsy or eBay offers numerous benefits for individuals looking to monetize their passion. These platforms provide a ready-made customer base, credibility and trustworthiness and valuable data and insights. By leveraging the features and resources offered by these platforms, individuals can effectively showcase their creations, reach a wider audience and ultimately turn their hobbies into a source of income. With the right strategies and dedication, individuals can do what they love and make money from it. So, why not take that leap and turn your passion into profit on platforms like Etsy or eBay?

INCORPORATING DIGITAL PAYMENT SYSTEMS FOR SMOOTH TRANSACTIONS

Incorporating digital payment systems for smooth transactions is crucial when turning your hobbies into a source of income. In today's digital era, people are increasingly relying on technology for their purchasing needs, making it essential for businesses to adapt to this shift in consumer behavior. By integrating digital payment systems into your business model, you can provide a seamless and efficient transaction process for your customers, thus enhancing their overall experience. Incorporating such systems can also help you streamline your financial operations, enabling you to manage your income more effectively.

One significant advantage of incorporating digital payment systems is the convenience it offers to both businesses and customers. The ability to make payments online allows customers to complete transactions from the comfort of their own homes or while on-the-go, eliminating the need for physical visits to the store or meeting face-to-face. This not only saves customers time and effort but also provides them with a sense of convenience and flexibility in how they interact with your business. By accepting multiple digital payment options such as credit cards, debit cards and digital wallets, you can cater to a wider range of customers and their preferred payment methods, ensuring that no potential sales are lost due to limited payment options. Another significant advantage of digital payment systems is their ability to enhance security and reduce the risk of fraud. Traditional payment methods, such as cash or checks, are prone to theft or loss, putting both businesses and customers at risk. By incorporating digital payment systems, you can minimize these risks by relying on secure and encrypted transactions. Most digital payment systems utilize advanced security measures such as tokenization and encryption to protect sensitive customer data, ensuring that their financial information remains safe and secure. This, in turn, fosters trust and confidence among customers, making them more inclined to engage in transactions with your business. Incorporating digital payment systems can also streamline your financial operations and enable you to manage your income more effectively. These systems often provide businesses with real-time reporting and analytics capabilities, allowing you to track and monitor your sales and revenue performance. With access to valuable data, you can gain insights into customer behavior, identify trends and make informed business decisions. Digital payment systems can automate certain financial processes, such as invoicing and reconciliation, saving you time and effort that can be better invested in growing your business. These streamlined operations help you maintain a clear and accurate financial overview, making it easier for you to manage your income and investment in pursuing your passion. It is important to note that incorporating digital payment systems also comes with certain challenges and considerations. You should ensure that the digital payment system you choose aligns with your business needs and objectives. With a wide range of options available in the market, it is crucial to conduct thorough research and evaluate the features and functionalities of each system. You should consider factors such as transaction fees, integration with other software or platforms and customer support to make an informed decision.

It is important to prioritize security and data integrity when integrating digital payment systems. Customers trust businesses with their financial information and any breach of security can severely damage your reputation. It is essential to work with reputable and reliable payment service providers that adhere to industry-standard security measures and compliance regulations. Incorporating digital payment systems into your business model is essential when monetizing your passion and turning your hobbies into income. By providing convenience to customers, enhancing security and streamlining financial operations, digital payment systems can significantly contribute to the success of your monetized hobbies. It is crucial to conduct thorough research, choose the right system and prioritize security to ensure a smooth and secure transaction experience for both your business and customers.

IMPLEMENTING DIGITAL MARKETING STRATEGIES

Another effective way to monetize your hobbies is by implementing digital marketing strategies. In today's digital age, having an online presence is crucial for success in any business venture. By leveraging various digital platforms and tools, individuals can effectively promote their hobbies and turn them into profitable sources of income. One important aspect of digital marketing is creating a compelling online presence. This starts with building a professional website or blog that showcases your hobbies and the products or services you offer. The website should have a visually appealing design, easy navigation and well-written content that effectively communicates your passion and expertise. It is essential to optimize your website for search engines to increase its visibility and reach a wider audience. To drive traffic to your website, you can employ various digital marketing techniques such as search engine optimization (SEO), social media marketing, content marketing and email marketing. SEO involves optimizing your website so that it ranks higher in search engine results pages, increasing its chances of being found by potential customers. This can be achieved by incorporating relevant keywords into your website's content, optimizing meta tags and improving site speed and mobile-friendliness. Social media marketing is another powerful strategy for promoting your hobbies and turning them into a source of income. By creating business profiles on popular social media platforms such as Facebook, Instagram and Twitter, you can connect with your target audience, share engaging content and drive traffic to your website.

Social media platforms also provide advertising options, allowing you to reach a wider audience by targeting specific demographics and interests. Content marketing involves creating and sharing valuable and relevant content to attract and retain customers. This can include blog posts, videos, infographics and e-books that showcase your knowledge and expertise in your hobbies. By consistently delivering high-quality content, you can establish yourself as an authority in your field and build trust with your audience. Email marketing is another effective way to engage with your audience and promote your hobbies. By collecting and building an email list of interested individuals, you can regularly send them updates, newsletters and exclusive offers related to your hobbies. This allows you to maintain a direct line of communication with your audience and ensures that they stay connected and informed about your latest activities and products. Digital marketing also includes using analytics tools to track and measure the effectiveness of your marketing efforts. By analyzing data such as website traffic, conversion rates and customer engagement, you can gain valuable insights into your target audience's behavior and preferences. This information can help you refine your marketing strategies, tailor your offerings to meet customer demands and optimize your website and content to drive better results. Implementing digital marketing strategies is essential for monetizing your hobbies and turning them into a source of income. Building a professional website, optimizing it for search engines and leveraging social media platforms are key steps in creating a compelling online presence. Utilizing content marketing, email marketing and analytics tools can further enhance your marketing efforts by engaging with your audience, measuring results and refining your strategies. By effectively implementing these digital marketing techniques, individuals can successfully promote their hobbies and generate income from doing what they love.

UTILIZING SEARCH ENGINE OPTIMIZATION TECHNIQUES TO IMPROVE ONLINE VISIBILITY

Search engine optimization (SEO) techniques are essential in enhancing the online visibility of businesses and individuals looking to monetize their passions. With millions of websites competing for attention online, it is crucial to implement strategies that improve search engine rankings and drive traffic to one's website. One effective SEO technique is the use of keywords. By conducting thorough keyword research, individuals can identify the specific terms and phrases that their target audience is most likely to search for. These keywords can then be strategically integrated into website content, meta tags and headlines to optimize visibility in search engine results pages (SERPs). Creating high-quality, engaging and informative content is vital for improving online visibility. Search engines favor websites that offer valuable information to users, so producing content that is relevant and helpful can significantly increase the chances of ranking higher in SERPs. Incorporating various types of media, such as images, videos and infographics, can enhance the user experience and attract more visitors to the website. Another essential SEO technique is optimizing website structure and navigation. Search engines prioritize websites that are easy to navigate and provide a positive user experience. Individuals must ensure that their website is well-organized, with clear and concise menus, headings and subheadings. Optimizing website loading speed is crucial, as slow-loading pages can negatively impact both user experience and search engine rankings. Backlink building is a crucial aspect of SEO that can significantly improve online visibility. Backlinks are links from external websites that lead to one's website. When reputable websites link back to an individual's website, search engines perceive it as a vote of confidence, boosting the website's authority and credibility. Individuals should focus on building a network of high-quality backlinks that are relevant to their niche and industry. It is essential to note that backlinks should be obtained organically, as search engines penalize websites that engage in unethical link-building practices. Monitoring and analyzing website performance is critical for optimizing online visibility. By utilizing analytical tools such as Google Analytics, individuals can gather valuable data on website traffic, conversion rates, bounce rates and various other metrics. This data can then be used to identify areas for improvement, adjust SEO strategies and maximize online visibility. Monitoring competitor websites can provide valuable insight into their SEO techniques and enable individuals to stay ahead of the competition. Search engine optimization techniques are crucial for improving online visibility and monetizing one's passion. By utilizing strategies such as keyword research, producing high-quality content, optimizing website structure and navigation, building backlinks and monitoring website performance, individuals can enhance their search engine rankings, attract more organic traffic and ultimately turn their hobbies into a source of income. With the ever-increasing competition in the online world, implementing effective SEO techniques is a necessity for anyone looking to succeed in monetizing their passions.

LEVERAGING EMAIL MARKETING AND CONTENT CREATION TO ENGAGE POTENTIAL CUSTOMERS

Another effective strategy to engage potential customers and monetize your passion is by leveraging email marketing and content creation. In today's digital age, email marketing continues to be a highly effective tool for reaching a wide audience and building relationships with potential customers. By creating a newsletter or subscription service, you can gather email addresses from interested individuals and send them regular updates about your hobby-based business. This allows you to stay top-of-mind and consistently provide valuable content to your audience. When it comes to content creation, there are numerous opportunities to showcase your expertise and attract potential customers. Whether it's through blogging, vlogging or creating social media content, producing high-quality and engaging content can help you establish yourself as an authority in your niche. By sharing valuable tips, tutorials and insights, you can build trust and credibility with your audience, ultimately leading to increased customer engagement and monetization opportunities. One effective way to leverage email marketing is by sending out regular newsletters that provide valuable content to your subscribers. These newsletters can include updates about your latest projects, behind-the-scenes looks at your creative process, exclusive discounts or promotions and tips and tricks related to your hobby. By consistently providing value to your subscribers, you can keep them engaged and interested in what you have to offer. You can also use email marketing to promote special events or products, driving sales and monetizing your passion. In addition to newsletters, you can also create an email autoresponder series that provides a more in-depth look at your hobby or niche. This series can be delivered over a period of time, providing subscribers with a comprehensive guide or course related to your expertise. By delivering valuable content and positioning yourself as an expert, you can further build trust and establish yourself as a go-to resource for potential customers. Content creation is another powerful tool to engage potential customers and monetize your passion. By consistently producing high-quality content, you can attract a loyal following and position yourself as an authority in your niche. Blogging is a popular form of content creation that allows you to share your knowledge and experiences with a wide audience. By regularly updating your blog with informative and valuable articles, you can attract organic traffic from search engines and keep readers coming back for more. Vlogging or video blogging, is another popular content creation method that can help you engage potential customers. By creating videos that showcase your skills, provide tutorials or share insights into your hobby, you can connect with an audience on a more personal level. Sharing your unique perspective and expertise through video can help build trust and establish a loyal following. Social media is another powerful platform for content creation and customer engagement. By creating and sharing visual content, such as photos or videos, you can attract attention and spark interest in your hobby-based business. Platforms like Instagram, YouTube and TikTok are particularly popular for sharing creative content and connecting with potential customers. By utilizing hashtags and engaging with your audience through comments and direct messages, you can build a strong online presence and attract followers who are genuinely interested in your passion.

Leveraging email marketing and content creation are two vital strategies to engage potential customers and monetize your passion. By building an email list and regularly sending valuable content to your subscribers, you can stay top-of-mind and drive sales. Creating high-quality content through blogging, vlogging and social media can help you establish yourself as an authority in your niche and attract a loyal following. With these digital tools at your disposal, you can turn your hobbies into a source of income and do what you love while making money from it.

Turning your hobbies into a source of income can be a dream come true for many people. The idea of doing what you love and making money from it is incredibly appealing. It's important to approach this endeavor with a clear plan and practical strategies. In order to successfully monetize your passion, you need to identify potential opportunities, create a comprehensive business plan and utilize digital tools and resources.

The first step in turning your hobbies into income is to identify opportunities that align with your interests and skills. Take the time to thoroughly research the market and explore different avenues where your passion can be monetized. For example, if your hobby is photography, you can consider becoming a freelance photographer, selling prints of your work or offering photography workshops. By identifying potential opportunities that are in line with your passion, you can begin to build a solid foundation for your business. Once you have identified potential opportunities, the next step is to create a comprehensive business plan. A business plan serves as a roadmap for your venture, outlining your goals, strategies and financial projections. It's essential to take the time to define your target audience, understand your competition and establish a pricing structure that is competitive yet profitable. A well-crafted business plan will also help you stay focused and organized as you navigate the process of monetizing your hobbies. In today's digital age, digital tools and resources have become invaluable in monetizing your passion. Utilizing various online platforms and social media can significantly boost your visibility and reach. Creating a professional website or online portfolio is essential for showcasing your work and attracting potential customers. Utilizing social media platforms such as Instagram, Facebook and Pinterest can help you market your products or services to a wider audience. By leveraging these digital tools, you can effectively promote your passion and generate income. In addition to creating an online presence, it's important to continuously refine and improve your skills. Stay up to date with the latest trends, technology and techniques in your field. Attend workshops, conferences and industry events to network with professionals and gain new insights. By constantly learning and evolving, you can position yourself as an expert in your field and offer unique and high-quality products or services. This will not only attract more customers but also enhance your credibility and reputation. When monetizing your passion, it's crucial to be realistic about the financial aspect of your venture. While it's possible to make a living from your hobbies, it may take time and effort to establish a stable income stream. In the early stages, it's advisable to have a backup plan or another source of income to support yourself financially. This will allow you to invest in your business without the pressure of immediately generating significant profits. As your business grows, you can gradually reduce your reliance on other sources of income and focus on expanding and improving your passion-based enterprise. Turning your hobbies into income is an exciting and rewarding endeavor. By identifying potential opportunities, creating a comprehensive business plan and utilizing digital tools and resources, you can effectively monetize your passion and make money from doing what you love. Remember to stay focused, continue learning and be patient with the process. With dedication and perseverance, you can turn your hobbies into a successful and fulfilling source of income.

V. OVERCOMING CHALLENGES AND RISKS

While the idea of turning one's hobbies into a source of income may be appealing, it is important to acknowledge and address the challenges and risks that come along with this endeavor. First and foremost, a major hurdle that individuals may encounter is the misconception that simply being passionate about something automatically translates into success. While passion is indeed a driving force, it is important to remember that transforming a hobby into a business requires careful planning, efficient execution and a solid understanding of market dynamics. One common challenge faced by individuals seeking to monetize their hobbies is the lack of professional experience in the chosen field. For instance, someone who has always had a passion for baking may face some initial struggles when trying to generate income from their skills. In such cases, it is essential to develop the necessary expertise by seeking out professional training, attending workshops and collaborating with experienced individuals. By investing time and effort into enhancing their skills, individuals can overcome this challenge and gain credibility in their chosen field. Another risk that aspiring hobby-turned-entrepreneurs should be aware of is financial instability. Transforming a passion into a business often requires a significant investment of resources, including both time and money. For instance, individuals may need to purchase specialized equipment, rent a studio or workspace or invest in marketing efforts to promote their products or services. It often takes time for a newly established business to generate a stable income. It is crucial for individuals to conduct thorough market research, develop a realistic financial plan and secure alternative sources of income, if necessary, to mitigate the risks associated with financial instability. Creating a sustainable business model is yet another challenge that individuals may face when monetizing their hobbies. It is imperative to strike a balance between creativity and commercial viability. While maintaining the unique essence of one's hobby is important, it is equally crucial to adapt to market demands and consumer preferences. For instance, an individual who loves painting may need to identify the types of artwork that sell well in the market and tailor their artistic style accordingly. By continuously monitoring market trends and customer feedback, individuals can refine their products or services to meet the demands of the target audience, thereby increasing the likelihood of success. The availability of digital tools poses both opportunities and risks for individuals seeking to monetize their hobbies. On one hand, the rise of e-commerce platforms and social media has democratized entrepreneurship, allowing individuals to reach a wider audience and promote their offerings to potential customers with ease. The digital landscape is highly competitive, making it imperative for individuals to develop a strong online presence and effective digital marketing strategies to stand out from the crowd. Embracing digital tools and staying up to date with technological advancements can give individuals an edge in today's interconnected world, while neglecting this aspect may hinder their chances of success.

The fear of failure can often discourage individuals from pursuing their dream of turning their hobbies into a sustainable income source. It is important to remember that setbacks and failures are an inherent part of any entrepreneurial journey. Success rarely comes overnight and it is essential to have a resilient mindset and perseverance to overcome obstacles and learn from failures along the way. Seeking guidance from mentors, connecting with like-minded individuals and regularly reassessing and adjusting business strategies can significantly contribute to overcoming these challenges and increasing the chances of success. While the prospect of monetizing one's hobbies may appear enticing, it is crucial to acknowledge and overcome the challenges and risks associated with this pursuit. Success lies in thorough planning, continuous learning, adaptability and a resilient mindset. By investing time, effort and resources, individuals can transform their passions into profitable ventures and find fulfillment in doing what they love while making money from it.

ANTICIPATING POTENTIAL HURDLES IN MONETIZING HOBBIES

Anticipating potential hurdles in monetizing hobbies can be crucial for individuals who are looking to turn their passions into a source of income. While it may seem like a dream come true to make money doing what you love, there are several challenges that can arise along the way. One hurdle to consider is the oversaturation of the market. With the rise of social media and the accessibility of online platforms, it is now easier than ever for individuals to showcase their hobbies and monetize them. This means that your chosen hobby may face stiff competition from others who are offering similar products or services. It is important to research the market and identify what sets your passion apart from others in order to stand out and attract customers. Another potential hurdle to anticipate is the need for continuous innovation and improvement. In order to successfully monetize a hobby, it is crucial to keep up with the latest trends and constantly offer something new and exciting to customers. This can be particularly challenging, as not only do you need to stay ahead of the competition, but you also need to consistently meet the ever-changing demands of your target market. This requires a keen eye for innovation, a willingness to adapt and a commitment to constantly improving your skills and offerings.

Time management is another obstacle that individuals may encounter when monetizing their hobbies. Transitioning from a casual interest to a business venture requires careful time management skills. When your hobby becomes a source of income, it is no longer just a leisurely activity but a commitment that requires dedication and a significant amount of time. This can be challenging, especially for those who are balancing their passion project with other responsibilities such as a full-time job or family commitments. Effective time management and prioritization are crucial in order to balance the demands of both your hobby-turned-business and your other obligations.

One potential hurdle that should not be overlooked is the potential for burnout. When a hobby becomes a job, it can sometimes lose its charm and begin to feel like work. This can be particularly true if you are faced with tight deadlines or high customer demands. It is important to find a balance between monetizing your passion and still enjoying it as a leisure activity. This may involve setting boundaries, taking breaks and finding ways to remind yourself of the reasons why you fell in love with your hobby in the first place. By taking care of your physical and mental well-being, you can prevent burnout and ensure that your passion continues to bring joy, both personally and financially.

Financial considerations are important to anticipate when monetizing hobbies. While the idea of making money from your passions may be enticing, it is important to recognize that there are financial risks involved. Starting a business, even if it is based on a hobby, requires initial investments, whether it be in materials, equipment or marketing efforts. It is important to assess your personal financial situation and determine if you have the resources to invest in your hobby-turned-business. You should also consider the potential fluctuations in income that may come with monetizing your hobbies. Unlike a steady paycheck from a traditional job, your income may vary depending on the demand for your product or service. It is crucial to have a financial plan in place that accounts for these fluctuations and provides a safety net for any unexpected expenses. Anticipating potential hurdles in monetizing hobbies is essential for individuals looking to turn their passions into income. By addressing challenges such as market saturation, continuous innovation, time management, burnout and financial considerations, individuals can navigate the path to monetization with greater success. While turning hobbies into income may come with its fair share of obstacles, with proper planning, dedication and a love for what you do, it is possible to create a fulfilling and profitable business.

LIMITED MARKET DEMAND OR COMPETITION SATURATION

Limited market demand or competition saturation can sometimes pose challenges when attempting to monetize your hobbies. While it is important to pursue what you love, it is equally important to understand the market dynamics that can impact the potential for generating income. One of the key factors to consider is the level of market demand for the product or service you plan to offer. If there is a limited market demand, it can restrict the potential customer base and make it challenging to generate significant revenue. This is particularly true for niche hobbies or specialized skills that may not have widespread appeal. Competition saturation can also present obstacles when attempting to monetize your hobbies. If there are already numerous businesses or individuals offering similar products or services, it can be difficult to stand out and attract customers. In such cases, it becomes essential to find unique selling points or differentiate oneself from the competition in order to capture a share of the market. When faced with limited market demand or competition saturation, it is important to explore various strategies to overcome these challenges. One approach is to identify untapped or emerging markets that may have a demand for your hobby-related products or services. Conducting market research and staying updated on industry trends can help identify potential opportunities in underserved areas. For example, if you are an artist specializing in a specific art form, you may consider targeting a niche market where there is a demand for unique and personalized artwork. By catering to a specific customer segment, you can position yourself as a specialist and differentiate yourself from the competition. In addition to exploring new markets, another strategy to overcome limited demand or competition saturation is to diversify your offerings. While your passion may lie in a particular hobby, it is essential to adapt and expand your range of products or services to meet the changing needs of the market. For instance, if you are a photographer specializing in event photography, you could offer additional services such as portrait photography or photo editing to attract a larger customer base. By diversifying your offerings, you can tap into different markets and attract customers who may not have been interested in your core hobby initially. Digital tools and technology play a crucial role in monetizing hobbies, especially in the current digital age. Leveraging digital platforms and social media can help overcome limited market demand or competition saturation by enhancing visibility and reaching a wider audience. Building an online presence through a website or social media profiles allows you to showcase your work, engage with potential customers and build a brand identity. Investing time and effort in creating high-quality content, whether it be through blog posts, videos or images, can help establish credibility and attract followers. Through strategic use of search engine optimization techniques and social media marketing, you can increase your visibility and attract potential customers who are searching for products or services related to your hobbies.

Another key aspect to consider when faced with limited market demand or competition saturation is the importance of continuous learning and improvement. Staying updated with industry trends, acquiring new skills and experimenting with innovative approaches can help you stay ahead of the competition and adapt to evolving customer preferences. Investing in professional development opportunities, attending workshops or collaborating with other experts in your field can help enhance your knowledge and skill set, making you a more attractive option for customers. By continuously evolving and offering something unique or different, you can create a competitive advantage and increase your chances of success within a saturated market.

Limited market demand or competition saturation can present challenges when attempting to monetize your hobbies. By adopting strategies such as exploring untapped markets, diversifying your offerings, leveraging digital tools and continuously learning and improving, you can overcome these challenges and turn your passion into a sustainable source of income. While the journey may require perseverance and flexibility, the ability to do what you love and make money from it is an attainable goal with the right mindset and approach.

BALANCING PASSION WITH BUSINESS REQUIREMENTS AND POTENTIAL BURNOUT

Balancing passion with business requirements and the potential for burnout is crucial when turning hobbies into a source of income. While pursuing one's passion can be fulfilling and rewarding, it is essential to acknowledge the realities of the business world and the potential pitfalls that may arise. One of the first steps in successfully monetizing a passion is identifying opportunities that align with one's interests. It is crucial to conduct thorough market research to determine if there is a demand for the product or service being offered. This research will help gauge whether there is a viable customer base and a potential market to sustain a business. Next, creating a business plan becomes imperative in outlining the necessary steps and strategies to achieve sustainable growth and profit. This plan should include detailed financial projections, marketing strategies and operational procedures. It is crucial to strike a balance between passion and business requirements in the creation of this plan. While passion can drive the initial idea, incorporating practical business strategies will help navigate the challenges of the market. It is equally imperative to stay true to one's passion and not be swayed solely by financial gain. Integrating the passions and interests that initiated the journey of monetization into the business plan ensures that the core motivation remains intact and provides a unique selling point. Once the business plan is in place, utilizing digital tools becomes instrumental in capitalizing on the potential of the online market. With the exponential growth of digital platforms, it has become easier than ever before to reach a wider audience and showcase one's products or services. Leveraging social media platforms such as Instagram, Facebook and YouTube can increase brand visibility, attract customers and build a loyal following. Having a well-designed website allows potential customers to browse through products or services and provides a platform to establish credibility. Search Engine Optimization (SEO) techniques should be employed to ensure that the website ranks highly in search engine results, increasing the likelihood of organic traffic. Integrating digital tools effectively amplifies the chances of monetizing one's passion and reaching a larger customer base. The pursuit of turning a passion into a source of income comes with the potential risk of burnout. It is essential to be aware of the signs of burnout and take appropriate measures to prevent it. Burnout can occur when the demands of running a business outweigh the enjoyment derived from pursuing one's passion. Establishing a work-life balance is crucial to maintaining mental and physical well-being. This may involve setting realistic expectations and boundaries, delegating tasks and scheduling downtime. Seeking support through networking or joining communities of like-minded individuals can provide a valuable source of advice, motivation and inspiration. Engaging in self-care practices such as exercise, meditation or hobbies unrelated to the business can help prevent burnout and maintain the passion that initially drove the desire to monetize one's hobby. Successfully turning a passion into a source of income requires a delicate balance between passion and business requirements. Identifying opportunities and creating a comprehensive business plan are crucial first steps. Utilizing digital tools effectively enables entrepreneurs to tap into a wider market and amplify their chances of success. It is essential to remain true to one's passion and not solely focus on financial gain. The potential for burnout should also be acknowledged and preventative measures taken to maintain mental and physical well-being. By striking this balance, individuals can monetize their hobbies and enjoy the benefits of doing what they love while making money from it.

DEVELOPING CONTINGENCY PLANS AND SEEKING PROFESSIONAL ADVICE

Developing contingency plans and seeking professional advice are essential steps when it comes to turning your hobbies into a source of income. While pursuing your passion may be exciting and fulfilling, it is crucial to have backup plans in case things do not go as expected. Developing contingency plans involves thinking ahead and coming up with alternative options that can ensure a steady income flow. This step requires a realistic assessment of the market, analyzing potential risks and challenges and identifying potential solutions. One important aspect of developing contingency plans is conducting market research. This involves gathering information about the target audience, competitors, industry trends and customer preferences. By gaining a deep understanding of the market, you can identify potential gaps and opportunities that can be leveraged to your advantage. This research should also consider potential challenges that may arise, such as changes in consumer behavior, economic shifts or technological advancements. By being aware of these factors, you can adapt your business strategy accordingly and minimize the risk of failure. Another aspect of developing contingency plans is diversifying your income streams. Instead of solely relying on a single source of income, it is wise to explore multiple avenues. For instance, if your hobby involves creating handmade crafts, you can consider selling them through different channels such as online marketplaces, social media platforms or even setting up your own e-commerce store. By diversifying your income streams, you can reduce dependency on a single channel and mitigate the impact of any unforeseen circumstances that may affect one particular platform or market. In addition to diversifying income streams, seeking professional advice is crucial for success in monetizing your passion. Professionals can provide valuable insights and guidance based on their expertise and experience in the industry. They can help you identify potential pitfalls, provide strategies to overcome challenges and offer suggestions for increasing profitability. Seeking professional advice can come in various forms, such as consulting with mentors, attending workshops or conferences or even hiring a business coach. These experts can offer an objective perspective and help you navigate the complexities of entrepreneurship. Professional advice can assist in creating a solid business plan. A well-crafted business plan is a roadmap that outlines your goals, target market, pricing strategy, marketing plan and financial projections. It serves as a blueprint for your business and provides a clear direction for growth and profitability. Seeking professional advice can help ensure that your business plan is realistic, comprehensive and aligned with industry standards. Professionals can also provide feedback on your business model, helping you refine your ideas and increase the chances of success. Seeking professional advice can help you stay up-to-date with industry trends and digital tools that can aid in monetizing your passion. In today's digital age, technology plays a significant role in marketing, operations and customer engagement. Professionals can provide insights on digital marketing strategies, social media platforms, website development, online advertising and other relevant tools that can help you reach a wider audience and boost your sales.

By leveraging these digital tools effectively, you can maximize your earnings and create a strong online presence. Developing contingency plans and seeking professional advice are crucial steps in turning your hobbies into a source of income. By conducting thorough market research, diversifying income streams and seeking professional advice, you increase your chances of success and reduce the risk of failure. Establishing contingency plans ensures that you have alternative options in case of unforeseen circumstances, while professional advice provides valuable insights and guidance to navigate the complexities of entrepreneurship. With these strategies in place, you can confidently pursue your passion, do what you love and earn a sustainable income.

CREATING BACKUP STRATEGIES TO ADDRESS POSSIBLE SETBACKS

Creating backup strategies to address possible setbacks is a crucial component when turning hobbies into a source of income. While pursuing one's passion, setbacks and challenges are bound to arise. With the right backup strategies in place, individuals can navigate these setbacks and continue to monetize their hobbies successfully. One effective backup strategy is diversifying income streams. Instead of relying solely on one avenue for income, individuals should explore multiple sources to ensure stability and security. For example, if a photographer primarily sells prints of their work, they could also offer photography classes or sell photography equipment to generate additional income. By diversifying income streams, individuals can mitigate the impact of setbacks in one area and support their overall income. Another backup strategy to address setbacks is maintaining a financial safety net. It's important to have savings or an emergency fund that can be tapped into during challenging times. By having a financial safety net, individuals can weather setbacks without experiencing extreme financial strain. This safety net can provide peace of mind and allow individuals to focus on their passion without the constant worry of financial setbacks. Networking and building a supportive community can be another valuable backup strategy. By connecting with like-minded individuals in the same industry, individuals can gain insights, advice and potential collaborative opportunities. When setbacks occur, having a network of supportive individuals can make a significant difference in finding creative solutions and getting back on track. Collaborating with others can provide alternative perspectives and fresh ideas that can help overcome setbacks. Being adaptable and open to change is essential when creating backup strategies for possible setbacks. In today's rapidly changing world, industries and markets can shift unexpectedly, resulting in challenges for individuals monetizing their hobbies. By staying updated with industry trends and being willing to adapt, individuals can quickly pivot and adjust their strategies to overcome setbacks. This can involve learning new skills, exploring emerging markets or leveraging technology advancements to stay relevant and profitable. Turning setbacks into learning experiences is crucial for long-term success. Instead of viewing setbacks as failures, individuals should embrace them as learning opportunities. When facing setbacks, it's essential to analyze the situation, identify the factors that led to the setback and implement changes accordingly. By taking a proactive approach to setbacks, individuals can continuously improve their strategies and avoid similar setbacks in the future. Reflecting on setbacks can also lead to personal growth and skill development, strengthening one's ability to overcome challenges in the long run. Backup strategies are vital for individuals looking to monetize their passions. By diversifying income streams, maintaining a financial safety net, networking, being adaptable and learning from setbacks, individuals can overcome challenges and continue to earn income from their hobbies. Cultivating backup strategies ensures stability and security, allowing individuals to focus on their passions rather than being immobilized by setbacks. The journey of turning hobbies into income is not without its obstacles, but with the right strategies in place, individuals can navigate these setbacks successfully and create a sustainable and fulfilling career out of their passions.

CONSULTING WITH MENTORS, COACHES OR EXPERTS IN THE FIELD FOR GUIDANCE

Consulting with mentors, coaches or experts in the field can be a critical step in turning your hobbies into a source of income. These individuals possess the knowledge and experience necessary to guide you on the path to success. Whether it is a mentor who has already achieved success in your chosen field, a coach who specializes in helping individuals monetize their passions or an expert in the industry who can provide valuable insights and advice, seeking guidance from someone who has been through the journey before can significantly increase your chances of turning your hobbies into a profitable venture. One of the key benefits of consulting with mentors, coaches or experts is that they can provide you with valuable guidance and advice based on their own experiences. These individuals have already navigated the challenges and obstacles that you may encounter along the way. Their insights can help you avoid common pitfalls and make informed decisions that will maximize your chances of success. Mentors, in particular, can be instrumental in helping you develop the necessary skills and knowledge to monetize your passion. A mentor is someone who has already achieved the level of success you aspire to and is willing to share their wisdom and expertise with you. They can provide you with guidance on everything from identifying opportunities in the market to developing a business plan and executing effective marketing strategies. By tapping into their knowledge and experience, you can fast-track your journey towards turning your hobbies into a source of income. Coaches, on the other hand, specialize in helping individuals transform their passions into profitable ventures. These professionals have a deep understanding of the unique challenges and opportunities associated with monetizing hobbies. They can provide you with personalized guidance and support tailored to your specific situation. From helping you refine your business model to providing accountability and motivation, a coach can be an invaluable asset in your quest to turn your hobbies into a source of income. In addition to mentors and coaches, seeking guidance from experts in your field can also be highly beneficial. These individuals possess specialized knowledge and insights that can help you gain a competitive advantage in the market. They can provide you with industry-specific advice on everything from pricing your products or services to navigating the legal and regulatory landscape. By consulting with experts, you can tap into their expertise and avoid costly mistakes that could hinder your progress. When consulting with mentors, coaches or experts, it is crucial to approach the relationship with a mindset of openness and receptivity. These individuals are investing their time and energy in guiding you towards success, so it is essential to remain coachable and receptive to their feedback. Be willing to ask questions, listen attentively and be open to constructive criticism. Remember that their guidance is meant to help you grow and refine your ideas, ultimately leading you closer to monetizing your passion. Consulting with mentors, coaches or experts in the field can be a game-changer when it comes to turning your hobbies into a source of income. These individuals possess the knowledge and experience necessary to guide you through the process, helping you avoid common pitfalls and make informed decisions. By tapping into their expertise, you can fast-track your journey towards success, refining your business plan and executing effective strategies. It is crucial to approach these relationships with an open mindset and be willing to listen, ask questions and receive feedback. With the right guidance, you can monetize your passion and do what you love while making money from it. In today's fast-paced and ever-evolving world, finding ways to turn your hobbies into a source of income has become increasingly popular. With the advent of digital tools and platforms, the opportunities to monetize your passion have skyrocketed. Whether you love painting, writing, playing an instrument or any other hobby, there are numerous ways to transform it into a profitable venture. By learning how to identify opportunities, creating a business plan and utilizing digital tools, you can successfully monetize your passion and do what you love while making money from it. The first step in turning your hobby into a lucrative business is to identify the opportunities available in your chosen field. Conduct thorough research to understand the current market trends and demands. Look for gaps or niches that you can fill with your unique skills and expertise. For example, if your hobby is painting, determine if there is a demand for your style of painting or if there are specific themes that people are willing to pay for. By understanding the needs of the market, you can tailor your approach to meet those demands and stand out from the competition. Once you have identified the opportunities, it is essential to create a comprehensive business plan. This plan will serve as your roadmap to success and help you stay focused and organized. Start by defining your goals and objectives. What do you want to achieve with your hobby-turned-business? How much income do you aim to generate? Setting clear and measurable goals will help you stay motivated and track your progress. Next, outline your target audience and develop a marketing strategy to reach them. Who are the people that would be interested in your hobby? Determine their demographics, interests and behaviors. This information will guide your marketing efforts, enabling you to reach the right audience with the right message at the right time. Utilize social media platforms, online marketplaces and other digital tools to promote and sell your products or services. Establish an online presence through a website or blog and leverage the power of search engine optimization to increase your visibility and attract potential customers. Don't underestimate the power of networking and collaborations. Seek out individuals or businesses who share the same interests as you and explore partnership opportunities. Collaborating with others can expand your reach, expose you to new markets and provide valuable insights and support. Attend industry events, join relevant online communities and engage with like-minded individuals. Building relationships and connections can open doors to new opportunities and accelerate your path to success. In this digital era, leveraging digital tools is essential in monetizing your passion. Take advantage of various online platforms and tools that are designed to facilitate and streamline business operations. For example, if your hobby is writing, use websites like Medium or WordPress to publish your work and gain exposure. Consider creating an e-commerce store on platforms like Etsy or Shopify to sell your handmade crafts or artwork. These digital tools provide a user-friendly interface, secure payment gateways and built-in audience, making it easier for you to showcase and sell your products or services. Make use of social media platforms to create a brand persona and engage with your audience. Share behind-the-scenes glimpses of your creative process, offer tips and tutorials and interact with your followers. Building a strong online presence will not only attract customers but also establish your credibility and authority in your field. Turning your hobbies into a source of income is not only achievable but also highly rewarding. By identifying opportunities, creating a business plan and utilizing digital tools, you can monetize your passion and make a living from it. Remember to conduct thorough research, develop a comprehensive business plan and leverage digital platforms to reach your target audience. By combining your passion with entrepreneurial skills, you can create a fulfilling lifestyle where you do what you love and make money from it.

VI. LEGAL AND FINANCIAL CONSIDERATIONS

When it comes to monetizing your passion and turning your hobbies into a source of income, there are several legal and financial considerations that need to be taken into account. While it may seem exciting to start making money from doing what you love, it is important to navigate the legal landscape and ensure that you are operating within the boundaries of the law. One of the first legal considerations is determining the structure of your business. Depending on the nature of your hobby-turned-business, you may need to decide whether to operate as a sole proprietorship, partnership, limited liability company (LLC) or corporation. Each structure has its own legal and tax implications, so it is crucial to consult with a legal professional or accountant to determine which option best suits your specific circumstances. In addition to choosing the right business structure, you will also need to consider trademarking and copyrighting your intellectual property. If your hobby involves creating unique products, designs or content, it is important to protect your work from being copied or used without permission. Trademarks and copyrights can provide legal protection and help you establish ownership rights over your creations. Again, it is recommended to seek legal advice to navigate the complex process of intellectual property protection. You should be aware of any specific regulations or licensing requirements that may apply to your hobby-turned-business. Certain industries, such as food service or health and wellness, may have additional health and safety regulations that you need to comply with. Failure to adhere to these regulations can result in fines, penalties or even the closure of your business. It is essential to research and understand the legal obligations involved in your chosen field to ensure compliance. Another pivotal aspect to consider is taxation. Generating income from your hobby will have tax implications and it is crucial to understand your tax obligations as a business owner. Depending on your business structure, you may need to register for an employer identification number (EIN) or collect and remit sales tax. Familiarize yourself with the tax laws and consult with a tax professional to learn about deductible expenses, record-keeping requirements and estimated tax payments to stay in good standing with the IRS. When it comes to financial considerations, creating a comprehensive business plan is critical. A well-crafted business plan outlines your goals, target market, marketing strategies, financial projections and more. It serves as a roadmap for your business and provides insight into its viability and potential profitability. A business plan will not only help you secure financing if needed, but it will also serve as a strategic guide as you launch and grow your business. Speaking of financing, it is crucial to consider the financial aspects of starting and running a business. While some hobbies may start as low-cost ventures, turning them into profitable businesses often requires initial investments. You may need to purchase equipment, materials or inventory, invest in marketing and advertising or cover other overhead costs. It is important to assess your financial situation and explore funding options, such as personal savings, loans, grants or crowdfunding, to support the growth of your business. In addition to financial planning, it is important to keep track of your business's finances and maintain accurate records. Implementing an accounting system will help you monitor revenue, expenses and profit or loss. Proper bookkeeping is necessary for tax purposes, financial analysis and making informed business decisions. You may choose to hire an accountant or use accounting software to streamline this process and ensure compliance with financial reporting requirements. Monetizing your passion and turning your hobbies into income requires careful attention to legal and financial considerations. Understanding the legal structure of your business, protecting your intellectual property, complying with relevant regulations and navigating the taxation landscape are essential steps to set yourself up for success. Creating a comprehensive business plan, securing financing and maintaining accurate financial records are vital aspects of building a profitable and sustainable venture. By attending to these aspects, you can confidently pursue your passion and turn it into a fulfilling and lucrative source of income.

REGISTERING THE HOBBY-BASED BUSINESS LEGALLY

Registering a hobby-based business legally is an essential step in monetizing your passion and turning it into a sustainable source of income. While pursuing your hobby may have started as a personal endeavor, transforming it into a business requires legal recognition. Registering your business not only lends legitimacy to your operations but also protects you from potential legal complications in the future. There are specific steps you need to take to ensure that your hobby-based business complies with all the legal requirements. The first step to registering your hobby-based business legally is to choose an appropriate business structure. There are several options available, such as sole proprietorship, partnership, limited liability company (LLC) and corporation. The choice of structure will depend on various factors, including your personal preferences, liability concerns and tax implications. Each structure comes with its own set of advantages and disadvantages, so it is crucial to thoroughly research each option before making a decision. Once you have determined the most suitable business structure, the next step is to register your business with the appropriate government authorities. This involves obtaining the necessary licenses and permits to operate legally. The specific requirements vary depending on the nature of your hobby-based business and the jurisdiction in which you plan to operate. Common licenses and permits include a business license, tax identification number and any industry-specific permits. It is crucial to familiarize yourself with the legal requirements in your area and comply with them to avoid potential penalties or legal issues in the future.

In addition to registering your business, it is essential to separate your personal and business finances. This involves opening a separate business bank account to manage all financial transactions related to your hobby-based business. Keeping personal and business finances separate not only simplifies accounting and tax reporting but also protects your personal assets in the event of legal issues or financial problems. Maintaining separate financial records allows you to accurately track your business income, expenses and profitability, enabling you to make informed decisions and effectively manage your business finances. It is essential to have proper insurance coverage for your hobby-based business. While it may seem unnecessary or costly initially, insurance protects you from potential liabilities and unexpected events that could have a significant impact on your business. Depending on the nature of your business, you may need general liability insurance to cover bodily injury or property damage, professional liability insurance to protect against errors or negligence or product liability insurance for businesses involved in manufacturing or distributing physical products. Evaluating the risks associated with your hobby-based business and obtaining appropriate insurance coverage is a crucial aspect of legally protecting yourself and your business. In addition to the legal considerations mentioned above, there are certain tax obligations you need to fulfill as a hobby-based business owner. Keeping accurate and organized financial records is crucial for proper tax reporting. Depending on your business structure, you may need to file annual tax returns, pay self-employment taxes and comply with certain employment taxes if you have employees. It is advisable to consult with a tax professional or accountant to ensure that you are meeting all the necessary tax obligations and taking advantage of any available deductions or credits. Registering a hobby-based business legally may seem daunting, but it is a critical step towards turning your passion into a profitable venture. By choosing an appropriate business structure, obtaining the necessary licenses and permits, separating personal and business finances, securing adequate insurance coverage and fulfilling tax obligations, you can establish a legitimate and successful business that is recognized by the law. Complying with legal requirements not only protects you from potential legal issues but also enhances your business credibility and ensures long-term sustainability.

UNDERSTANDING THE REQUIRED LICENSES, PERMITS AND REGULATIONS

One key aspect to consider when turning your hobbies into a source of income is understanding the required licenses, permits and regulations. While it may be exciting to pursue your passion and make money from it, it is essential to ensure that you are operating within the legal framework. This not only protects you but also establishes credibility and trust with your potential customers or clients. One of the first steps in understanding the necessary licenses, permits and regulations is to research the specific requirements based on the nature of your hobby-turned-business. For example, if you are planning to sell handmade crafts online or at local markets, you may need to obtain a business license or permit from your local government. This process often involves filling out an application, paying a fee and adhering to certain regulations. These requirements may vary depending on your location, so it is crucial to do thorough research and reach out to the appropriate authorities if necessary.

For certain hobbies that involve physical spaces or facilities, such as opening a bakery or a photography studio, additional licenses and permits may be required. These can include health permits, zoning permits or construction permits. Health permits ensure that your business operates in a safe and hygienic manner, especially when it involves food preparation. Zoning permits ensure that your business is located in an area that is designated for the type of activity you are engaging in, while construction permits are necessary if you need to modify or build a structure for your business. It is vital to understand these requirements and factor them into your business plan and budget.

In addition to licenses and permits, there may be specific regulations that you need to comply with in order to operate legally. These can include occupational licensing, product safety regulations or intellectual property rights. Occupational licensing may be necessary if your hobby-turned-business involves a specialized skill or profession, such as providing financial services or offering legal advice. It typically requires you to pass certain exams or meet specific educational requirements. Product safety regulations are particularly important if you are manufacturing or selling physical products. Familiarize yourself with consumer product safety standards, labeling requirements and any applicable testing or certification processes. Intellectual property rights should also be considered, especially if your hobby involves creating original works, such as artwork or music. Research copyright, trademark and patent laws to ensure that you protect your creations and respect the rights of others.

Understanding licenses, permits and regulations is crucial not only for legal compliance but also for building trust and credibility with potential customers or clients. Displaying your licenses and permits in your physical or online space can help reassure customers that you are operating within the law and meeting certain standards. It also ensures that you are transparent and accountable, further establishing your reputation as a legitimate professional. Understanding the required licenses, permits and regulations is a critical aspect of monetizing your passion and turning your hobbies into a source of income. Thorough research and compliance with legal requirements not only protect you but also build trust with your target audience. Remember to research and understand the specific licenses, permits and regulations based on the nature of your hobby-turned-business. Whether it involves obtaining a business license, health permit or understanding product safety regulations, taking the time to understand these requirements will set you on the path to success. Don't forget to display your licenses and permits to establish credibility, differentiate yourself from competitors and assure potential customers of your professionalism and commitment to legal compliance.

ESTABLISHING APPROPRIATE BUSINESS STRUCTURES (SOLE PROPRIETORSHIP, LLC...)

Establishing appropriate business structures is a crucial step when turning your hobbies into a source of income. There are various options available, such as sole proprietorship, LLC or limited liability company, partnership and corporation, each with its own advantages and disadvantages. It is essential to carefully consider these structures and choose the one that aligns with your goals and requirements. One of the simplest business structures for monetizing your passion is a sole proprietorship. This structure allows you to enter the business world as an individual without the need for additional paperwork or formalities. As a sole proprietor, you have complete control over your business and decisions. You are entitled to all the profits the business generates. There are a few drawbacks to this structure. Since you are the sole owner, you are also personally liable for any debts or legal issues your business may encounter. It can be challenging to secure funding or attract investors as a sole proprietor. Forming a limited liability company (LLC) offers certain benefits that protect your personal assets while providing flexibility in managing your business. As an LLC owner, you have the advantage of personal liability protection, meaning that your personal assets are separate from those of the company. This shields your personal wealth from potential business debts or legal claims. An LLC offers a pass-through taxation structure, where business profits or losses are reported on the owners' personal tax returns. This avoids double taxation, commonly seen in corporations. It is important to note that forming an LLC requires more paperwork and registration fees compared to a sole proprietorship. Partnerships could also be considered when establishing a business structure for monetizing your passion. In a general partnership, two or more individuals come together to start a business. This structure provides a shared responsibility and allows for a division of tasks, skills and capital. Partnerships are relatively simple and cost-effective to set up, as they require minimal paperwork compared to corporations. Like a sole proprietorship, partners are personally liable for the partnership's debts and obligations. It is vital to have a clear partnership agreement that outlines each partner's responsibilities and liabilities. Corporations are another business structure to consider, particularly if you plan to scale your business or attract investors. There are two types of corporations: C corporations and S corporations. C corporations are separate legal entities and provide owners with limited liability protection. Corporations have perpetual existence, allowing for easy transfer of ownership. A corporation can issue stock to raise capital and attract investors. Forming a corporation requires fulfilling certain legal requirements, such as registering with the State and establishing a board of directors. Corporations have a formal structure and are subject to more regulations and reporting requirements, which can result in additional costs and administrative burdens. Establishing appropriate business structures is vital when monetizing your passion and turning your hobbies into a source of income. The choice of business structure depends on various factors, such as personal liability protection, taxation, ease of formation, management flexibility and future growth plans. Sole proprietorships provide simplicity and control, while LLCs offer personal liability protection and flexibility. Partnerships allow for a division of responsibilities and capital, while corporations provide limited liability protection and access to capital markets. By carefully weighing the advantages and disadvantages of each structure and considering your specific needs, you can select the most suitable business structure to support your entrepreneurial journey and maximize the monetary potential of your passion.

MANAGING FINANCES AND BOOKKEEPING

Managing finances and bookkeeping are essential aspects of monetizing your passion and turning your hobbies into a source of income. When you start a business based on your hobbies, it is important to have a solid understanding of financial management principles and effective bookkeeping practices. By effectively managing your finances and keeping accurate records, you can ensure the financial stability and success of your passion-based business. One of the crucial aspects of managing your finances is setting a budget. Setting a budget allows you to track your income and expenses, ensuring that you have a clear understanding of how your business is performing financially. By determining your fixed and variable costs, you can identify areas where you can reduce expenses and increase profitability. A budget helps you to plan for future expenses and allocate funds, accordingly, providing you with a clear roadmap for your financial success. Alongside budgeting, it is essential to keep detailed records of your income and expenses. Accurate book- keeping enables you to have a comprehensive understanding of the financial health of your passion-based business. By diligently recording your income and expenses, you can identify areas of growth and areas that need improvement. Maintaining organized and detailed records will save you time during tax season and help you maximize your deductions. Whether you choose to use professional accounting software or track your finances manually, maintaining accurate records is crucial for a successful and profitable business. Another important financial management practice is tracking your cash flow. Cash flow refers to the movement of money in and out of your business. It is essential to keep a close eye on your cash flow to ensure that you have enough funds to cover your expenses and invest in the growth of your business. By monitoring your cash flow regularly, you can identify cash shortages in advance and take proactive measures to address them. Analyzing your cash flow allows you to make informed decisions about budgeting, pricing and managing your resources effectively. Effective financial management requires you to separate your personal and business finances. Mixing personal and business finances can lead to confusion, make it challenging to track your income and expenses accurately and even have legal implications. Opening a separate bank account and obtaining a business credit card will simplify your financial management processes and protect your personal finances. By keeping your personal and business finances separate, you can maintain clarity, ensure accurate financial reporting and minimize potential risks in case of legal or financial issues. As your passion-based business grows, it is important to develop a long-term financial strategy. This includes investing in the growth of your business, managing debt, saving for future expenses and planning for retirement. Developing a strategy helps you make informed decisions about your financial priorities and enables you to set achievable financial goals. Regularly reviewing and updating your financial strategy ensures that you stay on track and adapt to changing circumstances and market conditions. Effectively managing finances and bookkeeping are pivotal to monetizing your passion and turning your hobbies into a source of income. By setting a budget, keeping accurate records, tracking your cash flow, separating personal and business finances and developing a long-term financial strategy, you can ensure the financial stability and success of your passion-based business. Remember that managing your finances is an ongoing process that requires dedication and attention. With a solid financial foundation and the right tools and practices, you can do what you love and make money from it!

SETTING UP A SEPARATE BUSINESS BANK ACCOUNT FOR TRANSACTIONS

As you begin to monetize your passion, it is essential to establish a clear boundary between your personal finances and your business transactions. By opening a separate business bank account, you not only ensure accurate record-keeping but also streamline financial operations and maintain a professional image.

One of the primary reasons for setting up a separate business bank account is to maintain accurate financial records. When your personal and business transactions are intermingled, it becomes increasingly difficult to track and categorize expenses and income accurately. By having a dedicated business bank account, you can easily monitor and document financial activities related to your passion-based business. This will not only benefit you from an organizational standpoint but also prove helpful during tax season. When it is time to report your business income and expenses, having a separate account will simplify the process and help you avoid any potential discrepancies.

Having a separate business bank account helps streamline financial operations. As your passion-based business grows, you will likely have more transactions to manage. Having a dedicated account will allow you to keep business-related payments and receipts separate from your personal banking activities. This separation will make it easier to reconcile and track business-related deposits and withdrawals, thereby ensuring that you have a clear understanding of your business's financial health. It allows you to accept various forms of payment, such as checks made out to your business name, which may not be possible with a personal account. This flexibility is essential for creating a smooth and efficient financial workflow. Setting up a separate business bank account enables you to maintain a professional image. When customers or clients make payments for the goods or services you provide, they expect to do so in the name of your business. By having a separate account, you can easily deposit and process payments under your business name, projecting a more professional and credible impression. This professionalism extends beyond financial transactions. Should you decide to expand your business in the future, having a separate account will make it easier to secure business loans, apply for credit or establish merchant accounts to accept credit card payments. The separation between personal and business finances demonstrates your commitment to running a legitimate and transparent business, thereby enhancing your overall reputation in the marketplace. Setting up a separate business bank account is an essential step when turning your hobbies into a source of income. It ensures accurate record-keeping, streamlines financial operations and maintains a professional image. Separating personal and business transactions allows for easier tracking and categorization, which is vital during tax season. A dedicated business bank account simplifies and enhances the efficiency of managing financial operations as your business grows. It portrays a professional image and enhances your credibility in the eyes of customers, clients and potential partners. By setting up a separate business bank account, you lay a solid foundation for the successful monetization of your passion, allowing you to do what you love and make money from it.

TRACKING INCOME, EXPENSES AND TAXES ACCURATELY

Tracking income, expenses and taxes accurately is a crucial step in monetizing your passion and turning your hobbies into a source of income. When embarking on the journey of transforming your hobbies into a profitable venture, it is essential to treat it as a business from the start. Keeping meticulous records of your income and expenses will not only help you stay organized but also enable you to make informed financial decisions. By accurately tracking your income, you will gain a clear understanding of your revenue streams and be able to identify which activities are generating the most profit. This will allow you to optimize and focus your efforts on the areas that yield the highest returns. Similarly, meticulously recording your expenses is equally important. From the initial investment in materials or equipment to the ongoing costs associated with running your hobby-turned-business, tracking your expenses will provide you with a comprehensive picture of your financial health. By keeping a detailed record of your expenses, you will be able to identify areas where you can cut costs and maximize your profitability. Having accurate expense records will be immensely helpful when it comes to tax season. Tracking your expenses will ensure that you can claim all relevant deductions and take advantage of any tax incentives available to small business owners.

Speaking of taxes, accurately tracking your income and expenses will make the process of filing your taxes significantly easier and less stressful. When turning your hobbies into a source of income, it is essential to understand the tax implications and obligations that come with earning money from your passion. Keeping clear and accurate records will make it easier to report your income accurately and submit any required tax forms on time. This will help you avoid costly penalties and ensure that you are in compliance with all applicable tax regulations.

To effectively track your income, expenses and taxes, it is highly recommended to leverage digital tools and technology. Various software applications and online platforms specifically designed for small businesses can streamline the process of managing your finances. These digital tools allow you to easily record and categorize your income and expenses, generate financial reports and even automate certain tasks. Such platforms can assist you in tracking your inventory, invoicing and even integrating with your bank accounts for seamless transaction tracking. By utilizing these technological solutions, you can reduce the time and effort required for financial management, allowing you to focus more on the creative aspects of your hobby-turned-business.

Digital tools can also provide valuable insights into your financial performance. By generating reports and analytics, you can quickly assess the profitability of your activities, identify trends and make data-driven decisions. For instance, if you notice that a particular product or service is not generating enough revenue, you can use this information to modify your offerings or explore new opportunities. Having access to accurate and up-to-date financial information is essential for assessing the viability and potential growth of your hobby-based business. Tracking income, expenses and taxes accurately is a vital step in successfully turning your hobbies into a source of income. By treating your passion as a business and adopting proper financial management practices, you can effectively monetize your interests. Accurate tracking of income allows you to identify profitable revenue streams and optimize your efforts. Similarly, monitoring expenses helps you control costs and maximize profitability. Staying on top of your tax obligations ensures compliance and prevents any unnecessary penalties. Leveraging digital tools and technology can simplify the financial management process, providing valuable insights and enabling you to make informed decisions. With a solid foundation in financial tracking and management, you can confidently transform your hobbies into a profitable venture while doing what you love. Turning your hobbies into a source of income is a dream for many people. They long for the opportunity to make money doing what they love and fortunately, it's not just a fantasy. With the right mindset, skills and a bit of digital know-how, anyone can monetize their passion and turn it into a viable business venture. The key lies in identifying opportunities, creating a solid business plan and utilizing digital tools to maximize the potential for success.

Identifying opportunities for monetizing your hobby requires some creative thinking. It's about finding a niche in the market that aligns with your passions and capitalizes on your unique skills or knowledge. For example, if you have a knack for photography, you could consider offering your services as a professional photographer or selling your prints online. If you are an avid gardener, you could start a gardening blog or YouTube channel and monetize it through advertising or sponsored content. The key is to think outside the box and explore different avenues where your hobby can bring value to others.

Once you have identified a potential opportunity, the next step is to create a solid business plan. This plan will serve as a roadmap for your venture and help guide your decisions and actions. It should include a thorough analysis of the market, competition, target audience, pricing strategies and a marketing plan. Conducting market research and understanding your target audience's needs and preferences are crucial for the success of your business. Determining your value proposition and what sets your product or service apart from competitors will be essential in attracting customers. A well-thought-out business plan lays the foundation for a successful and sustainable business.

Digital tools play a crucial role in monetizing your passion. In today's digital age, there is a wealth of resources and platforms available that can help you reach a wider audience, build your brand and generate income. For example, social media platforms such as Instagram and Facebook can be powerful tools for promoting your products or services. Creating engaging content and utilizing relevant hashtags can help attract new customers and create buzz around your business. In addition to social media, e-commerce platforms like Etsy and Shopify provide a convenient and accessible way to sell products online. These platforms handle the payment processing, shipping and customer support, allowing you to focus on creating and marketing your products. Digital marketing techniques such as search engine optimization (SEO) and email marketing can help drive traffic to your website or online store, increasing your chances of making sales. Embracing digital tools can significantly enhance your reach and profitability. Monetizing your passion not only allows you to do what you love but also offers the potential for financial freedom and independence. It's important to approach this journey with realistic expectations and a strong work ethic. Turning your hobby into a business requires dedication, perseverance and continuous learning. You must be willing to invest time and effort into honing your skills, staying up to date with industry trends and adapting to changes in the market. Success won't happen overnight, but with hard work and determination, it is achievable. Monetizing your hobbies is a viable and exciting way to turn your passion into a source of income. By identifying opportunities, creating a solid business plan and utilizing digital tools, you can maximize the potential for success. It's important to think creatively, research the market and understand your target audience's needs. Embracing digital platforms and marketing strategies will help you reach a wider audience and increase your chances of making sales. It's important to approach this journey with realistic expectations and a strong work ethic. With dedication and perseverance, you can do what you love and make money from it.

VII. NETWORKING AND COLLABORATION

Networking and collaboration are essential elements for turning hobbies into a source of income. In today's digital world, connecting with like-minded individuals and businesses is easier than ever before. By networking with others who share the same passion or have knowledge in the field, individuals can gain valuable insights, advice and support in monetizing their hobbies. Collaborating with others can also lead to exciting opportunities for joint ventures or partnerships, further expanding the scope of one's hobby-based business. One of the most effective ways to network and collaborate is through online platforms and communities. Websites like Meetup, LinkedIn and Facebook groups cater to specific interests, allowing hobbyists to connect with others who share their passion. These platforms offer a wide range of opportunities, whether it's attending events, joining discussions or simply reaching out to potential collaborators. By immersing themselves in these online communities, individuals have the chance to build valuable relationships and tap into a wealth of knowledge and resources. In addition to online platforms, attending conferences, workshops and industry events is another powerful way to network and collaborate with others in the same field. These events provide an excellent opportunity to meet industry experts, establish connections with potential clients or customers and learn from those who have successfully monetized their hobbies. Engaging in conversations and

191

exchanging ideas during such events can spark creative collaborations and open doors to new business opportunities.

Collaboration can take many forms, such as co-creating products or services with other hobbyists or partnering with established businesses. By joining forces with individuals who possess complementary skills or resources, hobbyists can leverage their collective strengths to create unique and marketable offerings. For example, a photographer and a copywriter can collaborate to create an e-course on photography and writing, catering to a niche audience interested in both fields. By pooling their expertise, they can deliver a comprehensive learning experience and reach a wider audience. Collaborating with established businesses can also be highly beneficial. Many companies are eager to work with individuals who have a strong personal brand and a dedicated following. By approaching businesses that align with their hobby, individuals can propose mutually beneficial partnerships, such as product endorsements, sponsored content or even product development projects. These collaborations not only provide a source of income but also increase one's visibility and credibility in the industry. It is crucial to carefully select partnerships that align with one's values and interests to maintain authenticity and ensure a successful collaboration.

In addition to networking and collaboration, utilizing digital tools is vital for effectively monetizing hobbies. With the technological advancements of the past few decades, individuals can leverage various online platforms and tools to reach a global audience and streamline their business operations. Social media platforms like Instagram, YouTube and TikTok allow hobbyists to showcase their talents, connect with potential customers and build a loyal following. By consistently producing high-quality content and engaging with their audience, individuals can attract sponsors, sell merchandise or even create a paid subscription model to monetize their online presence. Digital tools also offer efficient ways to manage and market hobby-based businesses. E-commerce platforms like Shopify or Etsy provide individuals with user-friendly interfaces to set up online stores, manage inventory and process payments seamlessly. Project management tools like Trello or Asana can help hobbyists stay organized and collaborate with team members or freelancers, ensuring smooth operations and timely delivery of products or services.

Networking and collaboration are essential components for monetizing one's hobbies and turning them into a source of income. By connecting with others through online platforms or attending industry events, hobbyists can gain valuable insights, support and business opportunities. Collaborating with like-minded individuals or partnering with established businesses can expand the scope and reach of one's hobby-based business. Utilizing digital tools and platforms allows individuals to showcase their talents, connect with a global audience and streamline their operations. By combining networking, collaboration and digital tools, individuals can successfully monetize their passions and transform their hobbies into sustainable income streams.

BUILDING CONNECTIONS WITHIN THE INDUSTRY OR COMMUNITY

Building connections within the industry or community is crucial when it comes to turning hobbies into a source of income. This is because networking allows individuals to expand their reach, gain valuable insights and find potential business opportunities. When seeking ways to monetize one's passion, it is essential to connect with like-minded individuals who can provide support and guidance. By establishing connections within the industry or community, one can increase their visibility and credibility, opening doors to collaborations and partnerships. Engaging with the community can generate valuable feedback and new ideas for further monetization. Networking within the industry or community provides several benefits for individuals looking to turn their hobbies into income. It allows for the expansion of one's reach. By connecting with professionals already established in the field, aspiring entrepreneurs can tap into their networks and gain access to a wider audience. This can prove invaluable for increasing visibility and attracting potential customers or clients. Building connections not only expands one's reach but also enhances credibility. By affiliating oneself with reputable individuals in the industry, one can enhance their own reputation and be seen as a trustworthy and knowledgeable expert. When attempting to monetize one's passion, connecting with like-minded individuals provides valuable insights and guidance. By networking with those who have successfully turned their hobbies into income, aspiring entrepreneurs can benefit from their experiences, learn from their mistakes and gain valuable insights into the industry. These connections can offer guidance on various aspects such as pricing strategies, marketing techniques and customer acquisition. Through these connections, individuals can leverage the knowledge and experience of others to avoid common pitfalls and increase their chances of success. Building connections allows for potential collaborations and partnerships. Networking within the industry or community can lead to collaborations with other individuals or businesses who share similar interests or complement one another's skills. By joining forces, individuals can create unique and innovative products or services that have a wider appeal and greater market potential. Collaborations also provide the opportunity to share resources, reduce costs and pool knowledge and expertise. By working together, parties can combine their strengths and overcome challenges more effectively than they could individually. In addition to industry connections, engaging with the community can contribute to the monetization process. Sharing one's passion with the community not only generates interest but also provides valuable feedback. Engaging with potential customers or clients allows entrepreneurs to understand their needs, preferences and pain points better. This knowledge can then be used to develop products or services that cater directly to the target audience, increasing the chances of success. Community engagement also fosters loyalty and word-of-mouth marketing, as satisfied customers are more likely to recommend products or services to others. The community can serve as a source of inspiration for new ideas or monetization opportunities. By actively participating in forums, groups or events related to one's passion, individuals can gain insights into emerging trends, consumer demands or gaps in the market. These interactions provide a fertile ground for brainstorming and exploring new ways to monetize one's hobby. The community can provide valuable feedback and validation for potential ideas, helping individuals refine their concepts and make informed decisions about their monetization strategy. Building connections within the industry or community is essential for successfully turning hobbies into a source of income. Networking allows individuals to expand their reach, gain valuable insights and find potential collaborations or partnerships. By connecting with like-minded individuals, aspiring entrepreneurs can enhance their credibility, tap into new networks and learn from the experiences of others. Engaging with the community generates valuable feedback, fosters loyalty and provides inspiration for new ideas. By leveraging these connections and engaging with the community, individuals can increase their chances of monetizing their passion and turning it into a sustainable income stream.

ATTENDING RELEVANT EVENTS, WORKSHOPS OR CONFERENCES

Attending relevant events, workshops or conferences provides a unique opportunity for individuals looking to monetize their hobbies to gain valuable knowledge and skills. These events often bring together experts in various fields who can share their insights and experiences, offering attendees a wealth of information and ideas. By participating in these events, individuals can also establish important connections with like-minded individuals and potential business partners, further expanding their network and resources. Attending such events can provide individuals with a platform to showcase their work, receive feedback and gain recognition within their industry. This acknowledgement can be essential for building credibility and trust with potential clients or customers, thus increasing the likelihood of successfully monetizing one's passions. Through attending relevant events, workshops or conferences, individuals can access a wide range of resources that can aid in the development of their business plan. For example, workshops often provide hands-on training and guidance on topics such as marketing, branding and sales strategies. By learning these essential elements of business, individuals can gain a competitive edge and better position themselves in the market. Conferences, on the other hand, offer insights into current industry trends and market demands. This knowledge can be invaluable in helping individuals identify niche opportunities and develop successful business models. Events often feature guest speakers who are industry leaders, entrepreneurs or successful individuals who have already monetized their passions. Attending their talks can provide individuals with real-life examples and inspire them to take action and turn their hobbies into income-generating ventures. Aside from knowledge and skills, attending relevant events, workshops or conferences can equip individuals with the necessary digital tools to monetize their passion. In today's digital age, leveraging technology is essential for finding success in any endeavor. Many events offer sessions or workshops specifically focused on teaching attendees how to utilize digital platforms and tools effectively. For example, these sessions may cover topics such as social media marketing, website development, search engine optimization or e-commerce strategies. Learning how to harness the power of these tools can significantly enhance individuals' ability to reach a wider audience, promote their products or services and ultimately generate income from their passions. Events may provide access to industry-specific software or applications that can streamline business operations, manage finances or track customer engagement. Utilizing these digital tools can save time, increase efficiency and allow individuals to focus on what they love while still running a profitable enterprise.

Attending relevant events, workshops or conferences can also open doors for individuals to explore new possibilities and diversify their income streams. These events attract individuals from different backgrounds and industries, creating an environment conducive to collaboration and creativity. By engaging with professionals from diverse fields, individuals can gain new perspectives and insights that can spark innovative ideas. This interdisciplinary approach can lead to the discovery of untapped markets or unconventional revenue streams that individuals may not have previously considered. For example, a photographer attending a conference on entrepreneurship may find inspiration in partnering with a writer to create and sell personalized photo books, combining their skills and passions to generate additional income. The possibilities are endless when individuals have the opportunity to learn from others and explore new avenues at these events. Attending relevant events, workshops or conferences is a vital step for individuals seeking to monetize their hobbies. These events offer opportunities to gain knowledge and skills, establish connections and receive recognition within an industry. Attending such events exposes individuals to valuable digital tools and resources that can enhance their ability to turn their passions into profitable ventures. By participating in these events, individuals can broaden their horizons, explore new possibilities and diversify their income streams. With the wealth of opportunities and insights available at these events, individuals can acquire the necessary tools and inspiration to transform their hobbies into income-generating pursuits.

JOINING ONLINE FORUMS OR GROUPS TO CONNECT WITH LIKE-MINDED INDIVIDUALS

Joining online forums or groups to connect with like-minded individuals is an essential step in monetizing your passion and turning your hobbies into income. In today's digital age, the internet provides a vast array of platforms and communities where individuals from all walks of life can gather and share their common interests. By joining these online forums or groups, individuals can connect with like-minded people who share the same passion, exchange ideas and experiences and gain valuable insights into the monetization process. One of the key benefits of joining online forums or groups is the opportunity to network with individuals who have already successfully monetized their hobbies. These forums and groups often comprise individuals who have turned their passion into a full-time or part-time income source and are willing to share their knowledge and experience. Engaging with these individuals allows hobbyists to gain valuable insights, learn from their success stories and understand the challenges they might encounter along the way. Being part of these communities provides access to a vast network of potential clients, collaborators and mentors who can offer guidance and support. By building relationships with these individuals, hobbyists increase their chances of success in their monetization journey. Joining online forums or groups offers hobbyists the opportunity to collaborate with like-minded individuals. Often, turning a hobby into income requires more than just passion and skill; it requires a creative genius and diverse perspectives.

By engaging in these online communities, hobbyists can find potential collaborators with complementary skills sets that can help them bring their ideas to life. For example, a photographer looking to sell their prints online can find graphic designers within these forums who can help create a visually appealing website or marketing materials. Through collaboration, hobbyists can leverage each other's strengths and create products or services that are more marketable and enticing to potential customers. Consequently, the chances of turning their hobbies into a viable source of income increase significantly. The insights and knowledge gained through these online forums or groups are invaluable when it comes to creating a business plan. Often, monetizing a hobby requires formulating a clear strategy and setting realistic goals. By engaging with the community, hobbyists can gain insights into various monetization techniques, understand the potential revenue streams and develop a solid plan. These online communities offer a wealth of knowledge on topics such as pricing strategies, marketing tactics and customer engagement. Engaging in discussions and reading through informative threads helps hobbyists gain a 360-degree view of the monetization process, allowing them to make informed decisions and set achievable goals. Consequently, they can increase the likelihood of successfully turning their hobbies into a sustainable income source. Being part of these online communities offers a platform to showcase one's expertise and gain credibility in the field. As hobbyists actively participate in discussions, offer advice and share their experiences, they establish themselves as knowledgeable individuals within the community. This visibility not only increases their chances of attracting potential customers but also opens up opportunities for collaborations, partnerships or even invitations to speak at events related to their passion. By actively engaging with the community, hobbyists can build a personal brand and establish themselves as go-to experts in their field, thus expanding their income potential.

Joining online forums or groups is an essential step in the journey of monetizing your passion and turning your hobbies into a source of income. These communities offer unparalleled opportunities for networking, collaboration, knowledge exchange and visibility. By connecting with like-minded individuals who have already achieved success in monetizing their passion, hobbyists gain valuable insights and guidance. Through collaboration, hobbyists can leverage diverse skill sets and create marketable products or services. Engaging in discussions and informative threads equips hobbyists with the knowledge and expertise necessary to create a realistic business plan. Being an active member of these communities helps hobbyists showcase their expertise and build credibility, opening up further opportunities for revenue generation. Thus, joining online forums or groups is an essential tool for anyone looking to transform their passion into a profitable venture.

SEEKING COLLABORATION OPPORTUNITIES WITH OTHER BUSINESSES OR PROFESSIONALS

Seeking collaboration opportunities with other businesses or professionals is an essential step in monetizing your passion and turning your hobbies into a source of income. Collaboration can provide numerous benefits, such as expanding your reach, accessing new resources and learning from experienced individuals in your field. By partnering with other businesses or professionals, you can leverage each other's strengths and create a powerful network that can drive the success of your venture.

One major benefit of seeking collaboration opportunities is the ability to expand your reach. When you collaborate with other businesses or professionals, you tap into their existing customer base or network. This can help expose your products or services to a wider audience, increasing your chances of turning your hobbies into a profitable venture. For example, if you are a photographer looking to monetize your passion, collaborating with a local wedding planner or a fashion blogger can provide you with access to their clients or followers. This exposure not only helps you gain more visibility but also establishes your credibility as a professional in your field. Collaborating with other businesses or professionals can help you access new resources that you may not have on your own. For instance, if you are a small-scale jewelry maker who wants to turn your hobby into a profitable business, partnering with a larger retailer or distributor can give you access to their established supply chain and distribution channels. This can save you time, effort and money that would have otherwise been spent on building your own infrastructure. By consolidating resources, you can focus on what you do best - creating unique and high-quality products - while leaving the operational aspects to your collaborator. This synergy allows you to maximize the efficiency of your business and generate a higher income from your hobbies. In addition to expanding your reach and accessing new resources, seeking collaboration opportunities with other businesses or professionals also provides a unique learning opportunity. Collaborating with more experienced individuals in your field allows you to gain insights and knowledge that can accelerate your growth. These individuals have likely encountered similar challenges and can offer guidance or mentorship based on their own experiences. By learning from their successes and failures, you can avoid common pitfalls and make informed decisions that can propel your venture forward. Collaborating with professionals who are already established in their respective industries can also enhance your reputation and credibility. This affiliation can instill trust in potential customers or clients, making it easier for you to monetize your passion and establish yourself as a reliable and reputable provider of products or services. Seeking collaboration opportunities with other businesses or professionals is crucial in monetizing your passion and turning your hobbies into a source of income. Collaboration allows you to expand your reach, access new resources and learn from experienced individuals in your field. By partnering with other businesses or professionals, you can tap into their existing customer base or network, providing valuable exposure for your venture. Collaboration allows you to access new resources, saving you time, effort and money on building your own infrastructure. Learning from experienced individuals in your field can accelerate your growth and enhance your reputation. Collaboration is a powerful tool that can drive the success of your endeavor and help you do what you love while making money from it.

EXPLORING PARTNERSHIPS FOR CROSS-PROMOTION OR JOINT VENTURES

Exploring partnerships for cross-promotion or joint ventures is a valuable strategy for individuals seeking to turn their hobbies into a source of income. By collaborating with complementary businesses or like-minded individuals, one can leverage their collective resources and reach a wider target audience, leading to increased visibility and potential revenue generation. Cross-promotion involves promoting each other's products or services to their respective customer bases, while joint ventures entail pooling resources and expertise to create innovative products or services. Both approaches can be highly beneficial for hobbyists looking to monetize their passions. One key advantage of exploring partnerships for cross-promotion or joint ventures is the opportunity to tap into a broader customer base. Often, individuals pursuing a hobby-turned-business have limited access to customers who share their niche interests. By partnering with businesses or individuals in related industries, hobbyists can reach a wider audience that may be interested in their products or services. For example, a photographer specializing in nature photography can collaborate with a local eco-tourism agency to offer joint packages, combining their photography services with guided tours of scenic locations. This partnership not only exposes the photographer's work to a new demographic but also offers added value to customers seeking unique experiences. Partnerships can provide hobbyists with access to additional resources and expertise, which may otherwise be costly or time-consuming to acquire independently. For instance, a baker who wants to expand their online presence and start selling custom cake toppers could partner with an established online marketplace for handmade goods. This partnership would enable the baker to tap into the marketplace's existing infrastructure, customer base and marketing channels, saving them the effort of establishing their own e-commerce platform from scratch. The marketplace's expertise in online marketing and customer acquisition can significantly enhance the baker's visibility and sales potential. Partnerships can serve as a platform for knowledge sharing and skill development. Collaborating with other professionals or hobbyists in the same industry can provide valuable insights and guidance, which can help individuals refine their offerings and business strategies. By engaging in cross-promotion or joint ventures, hobbyists can learn from experienced entrepreneurs and develop a deeper understanding of market trends and customer preferences. For instance, a fashion designer specializing in sustainable clothing can collaborate with a fashion tech startup to incorporate innovative, eco-friendly materials into their designs. Through this partnership, the fashion designer gains access to the startup's research and development capabilities, accelerating their growth and enabling them to stay on the cutting edge of sustainable fashion trends.

Partnerships can enhance a hobbyist's brand image and credibility. By associating with reputable businesses or individuals in related fields, individuals can leverage the trust and goodwill already established by their partners. This association can significantly impact customers' perception of the hobbyist's offerings, leading to increased brand recognition and loyalty. For example, an aspiring musician can collaborate with a renowned music producer to produce and promote their first album. The producer's reputation and connections can help the musician gain recognition in the industry and establish themselves as a serious contender. Exploring partnerships for cross-promotion or joint ventures is a valuable strategy for individuals looking to monetize their hobbies. By collaborating with complementary businesses or like-minded individuals, hobbyists can tap into a broader customer base, access additional resources and expertise, enhance their brand image and foster knowledge sharing. These partnerships provide opportunities for increased visibility, revenue generation and professional growth. Whether through cross-promotion or jointly developing innovative products or services, partnerships can be a catalyst for turning one's passion into a sustainable source of income.

SHARING KNOWLEDGE AND RESOURCES TO ENHANCE GROWTH AND EXPOSURE

Sharing knowledge and resources is an essential component when it comes to enhancing growth and exposure in any field. In the context of monetizing one's passion, the exchange of knowledge and resources plays a significant role in turning hobbies into a source of income. By sharing what one knows and tapping into the resources available, individuals can open up new avenues and expand their reach within their chosen field.

One way in which sharing knowledge can enhance growth and exposure is through networking and collaboration. By connecting with others who share similar interests or have expertise in related areas, individuals can exchange ideas, learn from each other and potentially collaborate on projects that can generate income. Networking events, workshops and online communities are just a few examples of platforms where individuals can meet and connect with like-minded individuals. These interactions allow for the sharing of knowledge and resources, which can lead to new opportunities and broader exposure. The act of sharing knowledge and resources can also help in refining and improving one's own skills and understanding of their hobby. Teaching others what one knows requires a deep level of understanding and expertise in the subject matter. By teaching others, individuals are compelled to clarify their own thoughts and explanations, solidifying their own knowledge and expertise. This constant exchange of knowledge and feedback with others can lead to continuous growth and improvement, enabling individuals to excel further in their chosen field. In addition to sharing knowledge, the availability and utilization of resources are crucial when it comes to turning hobbies into a source of income. Resources can include equipment, software, funding and even mentorship. In today's digital age, there are numerous online platforms and tools available that can help individuals monetize their passion. For instance, an aspiring photographer can make use of online marketplaces to sell their photographs or collaborate with a printing company to create merchandise featuring their art. By tapping into these resources, individuals can leverage their skills and passion to create a viable business model. Sharing resources can also result in increased exposure and opportunities. For example, a group of artists may pool their resources together to rent a gallery space, allowing them to showcase their work collectively. By doing so, they not only share the financial burden but also attract a larger audience who may not have been familiar with their individual work. This collaborative effort can lead to increased exposure and potentially generate more income for all those involved. Sharing resources can also lead to the development of innovative and creative solutions. By combining different skill sets and resources, individuals can come up with unique offerings that set them apart from their competition. For instance, a group of musicians may collaborate with a graphic designer and a videographer to create visually stunning and professionally produced music videos. This multidisciplinary approach can enhance the overall product and capture the attention of a wider audience, ultimately leading to more growth and exposure. To conclude, sharing knowledge and resources is an integral part of enhancing growth and exposure when it comes to turning hobbies into a source of income. By networking, collaborating and teaching others what one knows, individuals can expand their reach and tap into new opportunities. Utilizing available resources and sharing them with others can result in increased exposure, innovative solutions and the development of a viable business model. Through the continuous exchange of knowledge and resources, individuals can monetize their passion and do what they love while making money from it. The ability to turn one's hobbies into a source of income is a dream for many individuals. Who wouldn't want to do what they love and make money from it? The good news is that it is not just a pipe dream. With the right mindset, strategy and utilization of digital tools, anyone can turn their hobbies into a profitable business venture. In this paragraph, we will explore how to identify opportunities, create a business plan and use digital tools to monetize your passion. The first step in turning your hobbies into a source of income is to identify opportunities within your chosen field. This involves conducting thorough market research to understand the demand for your particular hobby. For example, if you have a passion for photography, you must determine if there is a market for your services in your local area or beyond. This can be done by surveying potential customers, conducting competitor analysis and seeking feedback from industry experts. By identifying opportunities for your hobby to be monetized, you can take concrete steps towards turning it into a profitable venture. Once you have identified opportunities, the next step is to create a business plan. A business plan serves as a roadmap for your enterprise, outlining your goals, strategies and financial projections. This document will guide you through the process of monetizing your passion by helping you establish clear objectives and a concrete action plan. When creating a business plan, it is important to consider factors such as pricing strategies, target audience, marketing tactics, competition analysis and financial projections. By developing a comprehensive and well-thought-out business plan, you can increase your chances of success and effectively monetize your hobbies. In today's digital age, utilizing digital tools is crucial for successfully monetizing your hobbies. The internet has revolutionized the way businesses operate, offering endless opportunities for entrepreneurs to reach their target audience and generate income. One of the most effective digital tools for monetizing your passion is social media. Platforms such as Instagram, Facebook and YouTube allow individuals to showcase their hobbies and attract a large following. By consistently posting high-quality content and engaging with your audience, you can build a loyal fanbase that can be monetized through sponsorships, brand collaborations or selling your products or services. Having a strong online presence through a professional website or blog can further expand your reach and credibility, attracting potential customers and generating income. Another essential digital tool for monetizing your hobbies is e-commerce platforms. With the rise of online shopping, individuals can now easily sell their products or services to customers all over the world. Platforms such as Etsy, eBay and Shopify provide a convenient and user-friendly interface for entrepreneurs to set up their online stores. Whether you are selling handmade crafts, digital artwork or personalized services, e-commerce platforms offer a cost-effective and accessible way to reach a global audience and generate income from your hobbies. Digital tools such as online courses and mentorship programs can help individuals enhance their skills and expertise in their chosen hobby. By investing in continuous learning and acquiring new knowledge, you can elevate the quality of your products or services, differentiate yourself from competitors and command higher prices. Platforms like Udemy, Coursera and Skillshare offer a wide range of courses taught by industry professionals, allowing you to master new techniques and stay up-to-date with the latest trends in your field. Seeking mentorship from experienced professionals in your industry can provide invaluable guidance and insights, accelerating your growth and success in monetizing your passion. Turning your hobbies into a source of income is not just a distant dream. With the right mindset, strategy and utilization of digital tools, anyone can create a profitable business venture from their passion. By identifying opportunities, creating a business plan and utilizing digital tools like social media, e-commerce platforms, online courses and mentorship programs, individuals can successfully monetize their hobbies. So go ahead and pursue your passion, because with the right approach, you can turn it into a rewarding and profitable endeavor.

VIII. SCALING AND EXPANDING THE HOBBY-BASED BUSINESS

Scaling and expanding a hobby-based business is an exciting next step for any entrepreneur who has successfully monetized their passion. Once a hobby has been turned into a source of income, it is crucial to have a plan in place to ensure continued growth and profitability. One of the key factors in scaling a hobby-based business is to identify the target market and expand the customer base. This can be achieved through various strategies such as market research, advertising and leveraging digital tools. Market research plays a vital role in scaling a hobby-based business. By understanding the needs and preferences of the target market, entrepreneurs can tailor their products and services to meet these demands effectively. Conducting surveys and interviews and studying market trends can provide valuable insights into the target audience's purchasing behavior and preferences. This information can then be used to develop new products or services that align with the customer's needs, thereby expanding the business. In addition to market research, advertising is a powerful tool that can help scale a hobby-based business. By developing a strong brand identity and using various advertising channels, entrepreneurs can increase brand awareness and attract potential customers. Traditional advertising methods such as print media, television commercials and billboards can still be effective, but digital advertising offers more targeted and cost-effective options. Leveraging social media platforms, search engine optimization and email marketing can help reach a wider audience and generate more leads. Digital tools such as websites and online marketplaces are essential for scaling a hobby-based business. Creating a professional and user-friendly website provides a platform for entrepreneurs to showcase their products or services, share their story and engage with customers. The website should be optimized for search engines and mobile devices to ensure maximum visibility and accessibility. Using online marketplaces like Etsy or eBay can provide additional exposure and access to a larger customer base. Another strategy for scaling and expanding a hobby-based business is to diversify the product or service offerings. Once a successful product or service has been established, entrepreneurs can consider expanding their range to target different customer segments or cater to new needs within the existing market. For instance, a jewelry maker who specializes in handmade earrings can expand their offerings to include necklaces or bracelets. By diversifying the product line, entrepreneurs can attract a broader customer base and increase revenue streams. Scaling a hobby-based business also involves streamlining operations and optimizing efficiency. As the business grows, it becomes crucial to establish efficient processes and systems that can handle increased demand. This may involve investing in inventory management software, automating repetitive tasks or outsourcing certain functions. By streamlining operations, entrepreneurs can ensure that they are maximizing their resources and delivering a high level of customer satisfaction. Collaboration and partnerships can be instrumental in scaling a hobby-based business. By teaming up with complementary businesses or influencers in the industry, entrepreneurs can tap into new networks and gain access to a wider customer base. Collaborations can take various forms, such as joint marketing campaigns, cross-promotions or co-branded products. These strategic partnerships can help increase brand visibility and bring in new customers, enabling the business to scale more effectively. Scaling and expanding a hobby-based business requires careful planning and execution. Through market research, advertising and leveraging digital tools, entrepreneurs can identify opportunities and attract a larger customer base. Diversifying product offerings, streamlining operations and collaborating with other businesses can further support the growth and expansion of the business. By applying these strategies, individuals can continue to monetize their passion and turn their hobbies into a sustainable source of income.

EVALUATING GROWTH OPPORTUNITIES AND SCALABILITY

Evaluating growth opportunities and scalability is crucial when turning your hobbies into a source of income. It is important to assess the potential for growth in your chosen field and whether your business idea can be scaled up to meet increasing demand. One way to evaluate growth opportunities is by conducting market research. This involves studying the current market trends, identifying your target audience and understanding their needs and preferences. By gathering this information, you can determine the potential market size and whether there is a demand for your product or service. It is important to analyze the competitive landscape and assess the level of competition in your chosen niche. This will help you understand if there is room for your business to thrive and grow. Evaluating scalability is crucial to ensure that your business can handle increasing demand and expand over time. Scalability refers to the ability of your business to accommodate growth without sacrificing quality or efficiency. This includes assessing your production capacity, availability of resources and scalability of your business model. For example, if you are selling handmade crafts, can you maintain the same level of quality and production as demand increases? Can you source the necessary materials in larger quantities? These are important questions to consider when evaluating scalability. In addition to market research and scalability assessment, monitoring industry trends and technological advancements is essential for identifying growth opportunities. Industries are constantly evolving and it is important to stay up to date with the latest trends and innovations that may impact your chosen field. This can help you identify emerging markets, new customer needs and potential partnerships or collaborations. By staying informed, you can adapt your business accordingly and position yourself as a leader in your industry. Another aspect of evaluating growth opportunities and scalability is creating a solid business plan. A business plan is a comprehensive document that outlines your business objectives, strategies, financial projections and operational plans. It serves as a roadmap for your business and helps you stay focused on your goals. A well-crafted business plan can also attract investors and secure funding for your venture. It is important to include a section in your business plan that addresses growth opportunities and scalability. This section should outline your plans for expansion, such as hiring additional staff, investing in equipment or technology or exploring new markets. It should also detail the financial implications of growth, including anticipated revenue and expenses. By including this information in your business plan, you demonstrate to potential investors that you have carefully considered the growth potential of your business and have a clear plan for managing it. Leveraging digital tools is crucial for monetizing your passion and scaling your business. The digital era has revolutionized the way we do business and it provides numerous opportunities for entrepreneurs to reach a wider audience and increase their revenue. From e-commerce platforms and social media marketing to online advertising and analytics tools, there are countless digital tools that can help you grow your business. For example, creating a professional website and optimizing it for search engines can increase your online visibility and attract more customers. Using social media platforms effectively can help you engage with your audience, build brand loyalty and generate leads. Digital tools can provide valuable insights into your business performance, customer behavior and market trends. By leveraging these insights, you can make data-driven decisions and optimize your business strategies for growth. Evaluating growth opportunities and scalability is essential when turning your hobbies into a source of income. It involves conducting market research, assessing scalability, monitoring industry trends, creating a solid business plan and leveraging digital tools. By carefully evaluating these factors, you can identify opportunities for growth, plan for scalability and position your business for success. With passion, determination and strategic planning, you can monetize your hobbies and make a living doing what you love.

ASSESSING THE BUSINESS'S POTENTIAL FOR EXPANSION

Assessing the business's potential for expansion is a crucial step in turning hobbies into income-generating ventures. Once individuals have identified opportunities and created a solid business plan, it is essential to thoroughly evaluate the potential for growth and expansion. This assessment involves considering various factors, such as market demand, competition, scalability and available resources. By thoroughly assessing these aspects, individuals can make informed decisions and devise effective strategies for expanding their businesses. When assessing the potential for expansion, one significant factor to consider is market demand. Assessing market demand is essential because it determines the size and growth rate of the target market. Individuals should conduct market research to understand the needs and preferences of potential customers. By identifying the demand for their products or services, individuals can determine if there is a viable market to support expansion efforts.

Competition is another crucial factor to consider when assessing business potential for expansion. Understanding the competitive landscape is crucial for identifying opportunities and challenges. Individuals should analyze their competitors' strengths and weaknesses and identify any gaps that can be exploited. This analysis allows individuals to position themselves strategically and differentiate their offerings from competitors. Individuals should assess the barriers to entry and consider how competition may evolve in the future to determine if expansion is feasible.

Scalability is another key aspect to consider when assessing the potential for business expansion. Scalability refers to the ability of a business to grow without significantly increasing overhead costs. Individuals should evaluate whether their business model can be easily replicated and scaled up to meet increasing demand. This assessment involves analyzing factors such as production capacity, supply chain management and operational efficiency. If the business can efficiently handle increased demand without a proportional increase in costs, it may be more likely to succeed in expansion efforts. Assessing the available resources is also vital when considering business expansion. Individuals should evaluate their financial, human and technological resources to determine if they have the necessary means to support growth. Adequate financial resources are needed to invest in marketing, production capacity and infrastructure. Having a strong team of skilled individuals is also crucial, as they will drive growth and manage the expanded operations. Individuals should consider whether they have access to the necessary technology and systems to support the increased demand and streamline operations. Assessing the business's potential for expansion is a critical step in turning hobbies into income-generating ventures. By considering factors such as market demand, competition, scalability and available resources, individuals can determine if expanding their business is a viable option. Conducting thorough market research and understanding customer needs and preferences allows individuals to identify potential opportunities for growth. Analyzing the competitive landscape helps individuals position themselves strategically and differentiate their offerings. Evaluating scalability helps determine if the business can handle increased demand without incurring significant costs.

Assessing available resources ensures individuals have the necessary means to support expansion efforts. By carefully assessing these factors, individuals can make informed decisions and create effective strategies for expanding their businesses, ultimately monetizing their hobbies and turning them into a sustainable source of income.

IDENTIFYING NEW MARKETS OR CUSTOMER SEGMENTS TO TARGET

Identifying new markets or customer segments to target is a crucial step in monetizing your passion and turning your hobbies into a source of income. In order to effectively generate revenue from your hobbies, it is essential to understand who your target audience is and how to reach them. First and foremost, it is important to conduct market research to identify potential customer segments that align with your passion. This involves understanding the needs, preferences and existing gaps in the market that your hobby can address. By conducting market research, you can gain insights into the demographics, psychographics and behavior of potential customers, enabling you to tailor your offerings accordingly. Once you have identified your target market, it is important to create a marketing plan that effectively reaches and engages with your customer segments. This involves developing a clear value proposition that articulates how your hobby or passion can fulfill the needs of your target audience. Your marketing plan should also consider the various channels and platforms through which you can reach your customers. In today's digital age, utilizing online platforms such as social media, e-commerce websites and online marketplaces can significantly enhance your ability to reach and connect with potential customers. For example, if your hobby involves creating handmade jewelry, establishing an online presence through platforms such as Etsy or Instagram can attract customers who are specifically interested in unique, handmade products. In addition to understanding your target market and developing an effective marketing strategy, it is crucial to continuously adapt and evolve your offerings to meet the changing demands of your customers. This requires staying updated with the latest trends and consumer preferences within your niche. Innovation can be a powerful driver of success in monetizing your passion. By continuously exploring new ideas, experimenting with different products or services and seeking feedback from your customers, you can ensure that your offerings remain relevant and attractive to your target audience. For instance, if your passion is photography, staying updated with the latest camera technologies, editing software and photography styles can help you cater to the evolving needs of your customers and differentiate yourself from competitors. Another important aspect of identifying new markets or customer segments to target is understanding the competitive landscape within your industry or niche. This involves conducting a thorough analysis of your competitors – both direct and indirect. By understanding how other businesses or individuals are monetizing similar passions or hobbies, you can gain insights into potential opportunities or areas where you can differentiate yourself. This analysis can help you identify gaps in the market that your hobby can fill or ways in which you can offer a unique value proposition. For example, if you have a passion for baking, researching other local bakeries or home-based baking businesses can provide insights into potential customer segments that have not been adequately served. This can help you tailor your offerings to attract customers who are looking for unique flavors, dietary restrictions or personalized cakes. Identifying new markets or customer segments to target is a multi-faceted and crucial aspect of monetizing your passion and turning your hobbies into a source of income. By conducting market research, creating an effective marketing plan, continuously innovating and understanding the competitive landscape, you can position yourself to attract and engage with your target audience. Staying updated with the latest trends and needs of your customers can ensure that your offerings remain relevant and competitive in an ever-changing market. By taking a comprehensive and strategic approach to identifying your target market, you can maximize your chances of monetizing your passion and successfully turning your hobbies into a sustainable source of income.

DEVELOPING A GROWTH STRATEGY

Developing a growth strategy is essential when looking to turn your hobbies into a source of income. Once you have identified opportunities and created a business plan, it is important to have a clear strategy in place that will allow you to expand and make the most out of your passion. One of the first steps in creating a growth strategy is to identify your target audience and understand their needs and preferences. By conducting market research and analyzing your potential customers, you can gain valuable insights into how to tailor your products or services to meet their demands. This will not only help you attract new customers but also retain existing ones, which is crucial for long-term success. By understanding your target audience, you can also identify any emerging trends or unmet needs that present opportunities for growth. Another important aspect of developing a growth strategy is to set specific goals and objectives. By setting clear goals, you can stay focused and motivated, ensuring that you are moving towards the direction of growth. These goals can be both short-term and long-term, allowing you to have a roadmap for success. For example, you may set a goal to acquire a certain number of new customers within a specific time frame or to launch a new product or service within a year. Having these goals in place will help you prioritize your efforts and make strategic decisions that align with your growth objectives. In order to achieve sustainable growth, it is crucial to constantly innovate and adapt. The world is constantly evolving and so are your customers' preferences. It is important to stay ahead of the curve and continuously improve your offerings. This can look like regularly launching new products or services, staying up-to-date with the latest technology and trends and adapting your business processes to better serve your customers. By continuously innovating and adapting, you can differentiate yourself from competitors and maintain a competitive edge in the market. In addition to innovation, leveraging digital tools is another key component of a growth strategy. In today's digital age, there are numerous platforms and tools available that can help you reach a wider audience and increase your revenue streams. For example, you can use social media platforms to promote your products or services, e-commerce platforms to sell them online and digital marketing strategies to attract new customers. By embracing these digital tools, you can expand your reach beyond your local market and tap into new customer segments that you may not have been able to reach otherwise. Developing strategic partnerships can also play a significant role in growing your business. By collaborating with other businesses or influencers in your industry, you can leverage their expertise, resources and customer base to drive growth. For example, you can partner with related businesses to offer joint promotions or collaborate with influencers or bloggers to increase your brand awareness. Strategic partnerships can not only help you reach new customers but also build credibility and strengthen your position in the market. Developing a growth strategy is crucial when turning your hobbies into a source of income. By identifying your target audience, setting goals, continuously innovating, leveraging digital tools and developing strategic partnerships, you can position yourself for sustainable growth. Remember, monetizing your passion requires strategic planning, hard work and consistent effort, but with the right strategy in place, you can do what you love and make a living out of it.

SETTING REALISTIC GROWTH GOALS AND MILESTONES

Setting realistic growth goals and milestones is essential when attempting to monetize your passion and turn your hobbies into a source of income. Without clear goals and milestones in place, it becomes difficult to measure progress and stay motivated in the pursuit of generating revenue from something you love.

Aiming too high without considering the necessary steps and time involved can lead to disappointment and frustration, while aiming too low can hinder your potential for success. It is crucial to strike a balance between setting challenging yet attainable goals that can be measured through milestones along the way.

First and foremost, setting realistic growth goals ensures that you have a clear vision of what you want to achieve with your passion-based business. This involves taking the time to define your goals clearly, whether they are focused on generating a certain amount of income, reaching a specific customer base or expanding your offerings. By establishing a crystal-clear view of what you hope to accomplish, you will be better prepared to formulate a strategy that leads to success. Without these defined goals, your journey becomes haphazard and you may find yourself making decisions that are not aligned with your ultimate objectives. While it is important to have ambitious goals, it is equally crucial to set realistic milestones along the way. These milestones act as markers that indicate progress and provide smaller, achievable targets that serve as motivation to keep moving forward. By breaking down larger objectives into smaller, manageable tasks, you can effectively measure your growth and adjust your approach as needed. These milestones provide an opportunity for celebration and reflection, allowing you to evaluate what has and has not worked thus far and make necessary adjustments to continue on the path towards monetizing your passion. Setting realistic growth goals and milestones can help prevent burnout and discourage comparing your progress to that of others. When pursuing your passion and trying to generate income from it, it can be tempting to compare yourself to others who have already achieved success in your field. This comparison can be detrimental to your mindset and motivation, potentially leading to discouragement and feelings of inadequacy. By focusing on your own journey and setting goals and milestones that are specifically tailored to your circumstances, you are better able to maintain a positive outlook and remain motivated, even if progress seems slower than others. The process of setting realistic growth goals and milestones forces you to engage in thorough planning and strategizing. It compels you to consider various aspects of your passion-based business, such as market research, target audience identification and product or service development. Through this thoughtful evaluation, you can ensure that your goals are attainable within a reasonable timeframe and that the necessary steps to achieve them are clearly outlined in your business plan. This planning reduces the likelihood of unexpected obstacles derailing your progress and provides a solid foundation for future growth. Setting realistic growth goals and milestones enables you to build a sustainable and scalable business. By setting achievable targets and tracking your progress, you are able to make adjustments and improvements along the way that contribute to the long-term success of your endeavor. This process allows you to identify areas of growth, strategically invest in your business and create a solid reputation within your industry. By diligently working towards these milestones, you are more likely to achieve sustainable growth and turn your passion into a reliable source of income. When seeking to monetize your passion, it is crucial to set realistic growth goals and milestones. These goals provide you with a clear vision of what you hope to achieve, while milestones act as markers along the way, keeping you motivated and allowing for reflection and adjustment. Through this process, you can avoid burnout, resist comparing yourself to others, engage in thorough planning and build a sustainable business. By setting attainable targets and tracking progress, you can turn your passion into a reliable source of income and enjoy the satisfaction of doing what you love while making money from it.

ALLOCATING RESOURCES AND INVESTING IN NECESSARY INFRASTRUCTURE

Allocating resources and investing in necessary infrastructure are crucial steps in turning your hobbies into a source of income. Once you have identified the opportunities and created a business plan, it is essential to allocate the right resources to ensure the success of your venture. This includes both financial and non-financial resources. Financial resources may include the initial investment required to start your business or the funds needed to purchase equipment, materials or technology. Non-financial resources, on the other hand, may include your time and effort, as well as the skills and knowledge you possess. Investing in necessary infrastructure is equally important. This involves setting up the physical and digital infrastructure required to run your business. Physical infrastructure may refer to the physical location where your business operates or the equipment and machinery necessary for producing your goods or services. For example, if you have decided to turn your love for baking into a bakery business, you will need to invest in a commercial kitchen, baking equipment and packaging materials. If you have chosen to monetize your photography skills, you will need to invest in a high-quality camera, lenses, lighting equipment and a studio space. In addition to physical infrastructure, investing in digital infrastructure is becoming increasingly vital in today's digital age. This includes creating a strong online presence through a website or social media platforms. A well-designed website can serve as a virtual storefront for your business, allowing potential customers to learn more about your products or services and make purchases online. Social media platforms such as Instagram, Facebook or YouTube can help you reach a wider audience and showcase your skills or products through engaging content. Investing in the right digital tools is also crucial to monetizing your passion. Depending on your hobby, there are various digital tools available that can help you streamline your operations, manage your finances and market your products or services effectively. For example, if you are starting a graphic design business, investing in design software such as Adobe Creative Cloud can significantly enhance your design capabilities. Project management tools like Trello or Asana can help you stay organized and manage your client projects efficiently. It is essential to note that investing in resources and infrastructure should be done in a responsible and strategic manner. Conducting thorough research and careful planning will help you determine the most cost-effective and efficient way to allocate your resources and invest in necessary infrastructure. It is crucial to consider your budget, the expected return on investment and the scalability of your business. Starting small and gradually scaling up as your business grows can be a sensible approach, as it allows you to minimize financial risks while testing the viability of your venture. It is important to regularly assess and reassess your resource allocation and infrastructure investments. As your business evolves, your needs may change and it is crucial to adapt accordingly. Taking the time to analyze and understand the areas where you can optimize your resources and infrastructure will help you stay competitive and ensure the long-term success of your business. Allocating resources and investing in necessary infrastructure are vital steps in turning your hobbies into a source of income. By allocating the right resources, both financial and non-financial and investing in physical and digital infrastructure, you can create a solid foundation for your business. Careful planning, research and reassessment are key to ensuring an efficient and effective allocation of resources and infrastructure investments. By doing so, you can monetize your passion, do what you love and make money from it. Discovering how to turn your hobbies into a source of income can be an exciting and fulfilling journey. Many people dream of being able to do what they love and make money from it and with the right approach, it is indeed possible. To successfully monetize your passion, it is important to identify opportunities, create a business plan and utilize digital tools effectively. The first step in monetizing your hobbies is to identify opportunities within your chosen field. It is crucial to conduct thorough research to understand the market demand for your particular hobby. This involves analyzing the industry, identifying competitors and understanding the target audience. For example, if your hobby is photography, you may want to explore various avenues such as event photography, stock photography or selling prints online. By identifying the different possibilities within your field, you can assess which opportunities align best with your skills and interests. Once you have identified potential opportunities, the next step is to create a comprehensive business plan. A business plan acts as a roadmap for your venture and helps you stay focused on your goals. It should include a clear vision statement, a description of your product or service, target audience analysis, marketing strategies and financial projections. This plan will help you stay organized, set realistic expectations and demonstrate your commitment to potential investors or partners. It is essential to continuously evaluate and refine your plan as your business grows and market conditions change. In today's digital age, the importance of utilizing digital tools cannot be overstated. The internet offers numerous opportunities to showcase and market your hobbies. One effective way to monetize your passion is to create a personal website or blog. This provides a platform to share your expertise, showcase your work and attract potential customers or clients. By offering valuable content and engaging with your audience, you can establish yourself as an authority in your chosen field. Social media platforms such as Instagram, YouTube or TikTok can be powerful tools for promoting your work and reaching a wider audience. Building a strong online presence and actively engaging with your followers can significantly enhance your chances of success. In addition to online platforms, digital tools can also help in facilitating sales and transactions. For example, if you are an artist, you can use digital marketplaces such as Etsy or Artstation to sell your artwork directly to customers. These platforms provide access to a large customer base and handle secure payment processing, making it easier for you to focus on creating and marketing your products. You may also consider utilizing e-commerce platforms like Shopify or WooCommerce to create your online store. These platforms offer customizable templates, secure payment gateways and inventory management tools to streamline your online business operations. Another crucial aspect of monetizing your hobbies is building a strong network within your industry. Networking allows you to connect with like-minded individuals, potential clients and industry professionals who can offer invaluable guidance and support. Attending industry events, joining online communities and participating in relevant workshops or conferences can provide opportunities for networking. By actively engaging in conversations and sharing your expertise, you can enhance your reputation and attract new business opportunities. Turning your hobbies into a source of income requires careful planning, strategic thinking and the use of digital tools. Identifying opportunities within your field, creating a comprehensive business plan and effectively utilizing digital platforms are essential steps in the process. Establishing a strong online presence, building a network and continuously refining your approach will help you monetize your passion and turn it into a thriving business. With determination, hard work and a clear vision, you can truly do what you love and make money from it.

IX. BALANCING PASSION AND PROFIT

Balancing Passion and Profit is an essential consideration when seeking to turn one's hobbies into a source of income. While the idea of making money from doing what one loves is undeniably enticing, it is crucial to approach this process with careful thought and planning. It is necessary to strike a balance between pursuing one's passion and ensuring a sustainable profit. This balance can be challenging to achieve, as it requires an understanding of the market, adaptability and an ability to identify and seize opportunities. This delicate equilibrium necessitates the use of digital tools and a well-crafted business plan to effectively capitalize on one's hobby. To successfully marry passion and profit, one must first identify opportunities within their chosen hobby. This entails conducting thorough market research to determine the demand and potential profitability of the endeavor. While it is crucial to follow one's interests and passions, it is equally important to ensure that there is a market for one's products or services. This may involve identifying niches within the larger hobby landscape or catering to a specific audience that is not adequately served. For instance, if one has a passion for photography, they may consider specializing in a particular genre or offering unique printing services. Identifying opportunities alone is insufficient. One must also create and implement a solid business plan to ensure long-term profitability. A well-crafted business plan serves as a roadmap, outlining goals, strategies and potential challenges. It should include a thorough analysis of the competitive landscape, pricing strategies, marketing tactics and financial projections. By developing an effective business plan, hobbyists can transition from a casual pursuit to a more structured and profitable enterprise. This plan should be flexible to adapt to changing market dynamics and seize unanticipated opportunities. The integration of passion and profitability requires the decisiveness to make data-driven decisions and pivot when necessary. Utilizing digital tools is vital in monetizing one's hobby effectively. In today's interconnected world, a strong online presence is essential to reach a broader audience and generate income. Leveraging social media platforms, such as Instagram, Facebook or YouTube, allows hobbyists to showcase their work, engage with potential customers and build a loyal following. Through engaging content creation and effective digital marketing strategies, one can maximize their online presence and increase their chances of success. Online marketplaces and e-commerce platforms provide opportunities to sell products or services directly to consumers, eliminating the need for intermediaries and increasing profit margins. Digital tools can empower hobbyists to diversify their income streams by exploring various monetization avenues. For instance, in the realm of content creation, individuals can generate income through advertising, brand partnerships, merchandise sales or even crowdfunding. By combining multiple revenue streams, hobbyists can minimize risks and capitalize on a range of opportunities. This diversification also allows for creative freedom and the ability to continue pursuing the hobby passionately, as it alleviates the pressure of relying solely on a single income source. Striking a balance between passion and profit is essential when seeking to monetize one's hobbies. This equilibrium requires carefully identifying opportunities, developing a comprehensive business plan and utilizing digital tools effectively. By conducting thorough market research, understanding the competitive landscape and properly positioning oneself within the market, hobbyists can increase their chances of success. The integration of passion and profitability necessitates strategic decision-making, adaptability and a willingness to embrace new opportunities. Leveraging digital tools, such as social media platforms and e-commerce platforms, enables individuals to reach a broader audience, diversify their income streams and maximize their chances of converting their hobbies into a sustainable source of income. By finding the delicate balance between passion and profit, one can embark on a fulfilling and lucrative journey of turning their hobbies into income.

REFLECTING ON THE EVOLVING RELATIONSHIP BETWEEN PASSION AND INCOME

The evolving relationship between passion and income has long been a subject of interest and discussion. In today's society, it is becoming increasingly common for individuals to seek ways to monetize their hobbies and turn their passions into a source of income. With the rise of digital tools and online platforms, the avenues for doing so have expanded, providing individuals with greater opportunities to pursue their passions while also making money from them. One key aspect of this evolving relationship is the notion of identifying opportunities. In the past, individuals may have been limited in their ability to capitalize on their passions due to a lack of knowledge or resources. With the advent of the internet and various online platforms, individuals now have the ability to research and identify potential opportunities in their respective fields of interest. Whether it be through social media, online marketplaces or specialized platforms, individuals can connect with others who share similar passions and explore ways in which they can turn their hobbies into income-generating ventures. Creating a business plan is another crucial step in monetizing one's passion. While the idea of turning a hobby into a business may seem exciting, it is important to approach it with the same level of planning and strategy as any other entrepreneurial endeavor. A solid business plan helps individuals outline their goals, target audience, marketing strategies and financial projections. By mapping out these key elements, individuals can not only gain a clearer understanding of the feasibility of their passion project but also ensure that they are taking the necessary steps to make it financially viable. The role of digital tools in monetizing passions cannot be understated. In today's technologically advanced world, the internet has revolutionized the way individuals can turn their hobbies into income. From creating an online store to offering virtual consultations or even providing digital products or services, the possibilities are virtually endless. Social media platforms, for instance, allow individuals to showcase their talents or products to a wide audience. With the ability to reach potential customers from all corners of the globe, individuals now have the opportunity to create an online presence and gain customers that would have been otherwise unattainable. There are various digital tools and software available that can streamline business operations, such as project management apps, online payment systems and website builders. These tools not only enhance productivity and efficiency but also enable individuals to focus on their craft and passion, as opposed to spending excessive time on administrative tasks. It is essential to recognize that monetizing one's passion may come with its own set of challenges. While the idea of making money doing what one loves is enticing, it is important to acknowledge that the transition from hobby to income-generating venture may require a significant investment of time, effort and resources. It may take time to build a customer base, establish a reputation and generate consistent income. There may be financial risks involved, such as startup costs, marketing expenses or fluctuations in demand. It is crucial for individuals to be prepared for these challenges and approach the process with a realistic mindset. The evolving relationship between passion and income highlights the increasing desire for individuals to monetize their hobbies and turn them into income-generating ventures. Through the identification of opportunities, the creation of a business plan and the utilization of digital tools, individuals now have greater avenues to pursue their passions while also making money from them. It is important to approach this process with careful planning, recognizing that challenges and risks may arise. By doing so, individuals can embark on a journey that combines their love for their hobbies with the fulfillment of financial success.

ACKNOWLEDGING THE POTENTIAL IMPACT ON THE HOBBY'S ENJOYMENT

While the idea of turning one's hobby into a source of income may initially seem like a dream come true, it is important for individuals to acknowledge the potential impact on the enjoyment of their beloved hobby. Engaging in a hobby often brings a sense of peace and relaxation, allowing individuals to escape from the stresses of everyday life. The moment monetization is introduced, a new set of responsibilities and expectations come into play, which may potentially change the entire dynamic of the hobby. One of the main concerns when turning a hobby into a source of income is the potential for burnout. What was once an enjoyable pastime might start to feel like just another job. The passion and excitement that initially drew individuals to their hobby can easily diminish when it becomes a means of making money. The pressure of meeting client expectations, deadlines and financial goals can begin to outweigh the pure joy and satisfaction that the hobby itself used to bring.

The process of monetizing a hobby often requires individuals to turn their focus from purely creative or leisure activities to more business-oriented tasks. This shift in mindset, while necessary for entrepreneurial success, may also lead to a depletion of the enjoyment derived from the hobby. Instead of solely focusing on the creative process, individuals may find themselves consumed by marketing strategies, financial calculations and customer relations. As a result, the hobby itself may become overshadowed by the business aspects, ultimately detracting from the overall pleasure and satisfaction. When a hobby is monetized, individuals may feel compelled to create products or services that fit the demands of the market, rather than simply pursuing their own interests and passions. The pursuit of profit may cause individuals to compromise their artistic integrity, leading to a decline in quality or a shift away from the original essence of the hobby. This deviation from the core values and creative freedom that attracted individuals to the hobby in the first place may lead to a sense of dissatisfaction and loss of enjoyment.

The monetization of a hobby can also bring about positive changes, allowing individuals to explore new avenues of growth and personal development. By turning a hobby into a source of income, individuals can gain valuable skills, expand their network and open doors to new opportunities. The financial stability that comes with monetization can also provide individuals with the freedom and resources to further invest in their hobby, whether it be through purchasing higher quality materials, attending workshops or exploring new techniques. This increased dedication and investment in the hobby may enhance their overall enjoyment and satisfaction. Whether the impact of monetizing a hobby on its enjoyment is positive or negative depends on the individual and their ability to navigate the challenges that come with it. It is crucial for individuals to carefully consider the potential consequences and weigh the advantages against the disadvantages. By setting realistic expectations, establishing boundaries and finding a balance between the business side and the creative side of their hobby, individuals can mitigate the potential negative impact and ensure that their passion remains an enjoyable and fulfilling endeavor.

FINDING WAYS TO MAINTAIN ENTHUSIASM AND PREVENT BURNOUT

Maintaining enthusiasm and preventing burnout are crucial aspects when turning hobbies into a source of income. While it may seem like a dream to make money from doing what you love, it can also become overwhelming and lead to burnout if not managed properly. Finding ways to maintain enthusiasm and prevent burnout becomes essential in this process. One effective strategy to maintain enthusiasm is to set realistic goals and expectations. When embarking on the journey of turning a hobby into a profitable venture, it is easy to get carried away and set unrealistic expectations of immediate success. This can quickly lead to frustration and disappointment. Instead, setting achievable and measurable goals can help maintain enthusiasm. By breaking down the process and focusing on smaller milestones, individuals can see progress and feel motivated to continue pursuing their passion. Celebrating these small victories can provide a sense of accomplishment and keep the enthusiasm alive.

In addition to setting realistic goals, it is essential to stay connected with the initial passion that drove individuals to monetize their hobbies. Often, when hobbies become a source of income, the sheer pressure of making money can overshadow the joy that initially sparked the interest. To prevent this from happening, individuals should regularly remind themselves why they enjoyed their hobby in the first place. Rediscovering the initial excitement and finding ways to incorporate it into the monetized version of the hobby can help maintain enthusiasm. Avoiding burnout requires finding a balance between work and relaxation. When a hobby becomes a business, it is easy to become consumed by it. Overexerting oneself without taking breaks can lead to burnout. To prevent this, it is crucial to set boundaries and establish a healthy work-life balance. This includes allocating specific time for work and leisure activities, as well as taking regular breaks throughout the day. By setting aside time for relaxation and self-care, individuals can recharge their energy and prevent burnout from occurring. Seeking support from like-minded individuals can also contribute to maintaining enthusiasm and preventing burnout. Often, pursuing a hobby as a business can be a solitary endeavor, as individuals may primarily work alone. This isolation can lead to feelings of loneliness and decrease motivation. To combat this, joining communities or networking with others who share similar interests can provide a sense of belonging and support. Engaging in discussions with peers, attending workshops or conferences or even finding a mentor can help individuals stay motivated and inspired. Sharing experiences, learning from others and receiving emotional support can go a long way in maintaining enthusiasm. Embracing continuous learning and growth is vital to prevent burnout. Even when turning a hobby into a business, it is crucial to challenge oneself and seek new opportunities for growth. Stagnation can quickly lead to boredom and eventually burnout. Individuals should constantly seek ways to improve their skills, explore new aspects of their hobby and embrace change. This can be achieved by attending workshops, taking online courses or engaging in collaborations with other professionals. By investing in personal and professional growth, individuals can remain enthusiastic about their hobby and prevent burnout. Maintaining enthusiasm and preventing burnout are crucial when turning a hobby into a source of income. Setting realistic goals, staying connected with the initial passion, finding a balance between work and relaxation, seeking support from like-minded individuals and embracing continuous learning are effective strategies to achieve this. By implementing these strategies, individuals can sustain their enthusiasm and prevent burnout, ensuring their journey of monetizing their passion remains enjoyable and fulfilling.

SETTING BOUNDARIES AND MANAGING TIME EFFECTIVELY

These are crucial elements when it comes to turning your hobbies into a source of income. While pursuing your passion can be fulfilling, it is important to establish clear boundaries to avoid burnout and maintain a healthy work-life balance. First and foremost, it is essential to set realistic goals and expectations for yourself. Many individuals make the mistake of diving head-first into their hobbies turned business ventures without considering the time and effort required. By setting specific, measurable, achievable, relevant and time-bound (SMART) goals, you can outline your milestones and stay on track. This will enable you to manage your time effectively by allocating specific periods for work, leisure and personal commitments. It is crucial to establish boundaries with your clients or customers. While you may be passionate about your hobby, it is important to maintain professionalism and avoid becoming a 24/7 service provider. Clearly specify your working hours, response times and availability to your clients. This will prevent any potential misunderstandings and allow you to maintain a healthy balance between work and personal life. Setting boundaries will also enable you to allocate time for personal growth, skill development and research within your chosen field, which is essential for long-term success. Utilizing time management techniques can greatly enhance your productivity and efficiency. One widely practiced method is the Pomodoro Technique, which involves working in

25-minute increments followed by a short break. This technique helps in maintaining focus and preventing burnout.

Another useful strategy is creating a schedule or to-do list at the beginning of each day or week. By prioritizing tasks and allotting specific time frames for each, you can ensure that you stay organized and on top of your commitments. Minimizing distractions such as social media notifications or unrelated tasks can also help you stay focused and make the most of your time. Consider using tools like website blockers, time-tracking apps or productivity apps to keep yourself accountable and maximize your efficiency. In addition to setting boundaries and managing time, it is essential to continuously evaluate and reassess your progress and strategies. By regularly reviewing your goals and performance, you can identify areas for improvement and make necessary adjustments. This could mean seeking feedback from clients or customers, analyzing market trends or experimenting with different marketing strategies. Remaining adaptable and open to change is crucial when turning your hobbies into a source of income, as it allows you to stay ahead in an ever-evolving business landscape. Building a support network and seeking guidance from industry professionals can greatly contribute to your success. Connect with like-minded individuals through networking events, online communities or industry-specific forums. Engaging in meaningful conversations and sharing experiences with others who have turned their hobbies into successful businesses can provide valuable insights and inspiration. Considering a mentorship program or seeking guidance from a business coach or consultant can offer expert advice tailored to your specific needs and goals. Setting boundaries and effectively managing your time are essential components of turning your hobbies into a source of income. By establishing clear goals, boundaries with clients and utilizing time management techniques, you can maximize your productivity and maintain a healthy work-life balance. Continuous evaluation and adaptation, along with building a support network, will help you stay competitive and evolve in your chosen field. With a strategic approach and dedication, you can monetize your passion and transform your hobbies into a fulfilling and profitable venture.

ESTABLISHING WORK-LIFE BALANCE TO AVOID OVERWORKING OR NEGLECTING PERSONAL LIFE

The pursuit of turning one's hobbies into a source of income has become increasingly popular in today's society. Many individuals are seeking ways to combine their passion with their career in order to find fulfillment and financial success. It is crucial to establish a healthy work-life balance in this pursuit to avoid overworking and neglecting one's personal life. Failing to maintain this balance can lead to burnout, decreased productivity and strained relationships. By prioritizing self-care and setting boundaries, individuals can create a harmonious integration of work and personal life. One of the main reasons why it is important to establish a work-life balance when monetizing hobbies is to prevent overworking. When individuals turn their hobbies into a source of income, it can be easy to become consumed by work. The boundaries between work and personal life can become blurred, leading to excessive work hours and neglect of other important aspects of life. This can have detrimental effects on an individual's physical and mental well-being. Overworking can lead to burnout, a state of chronic exhaustion characterized by physical and emotional fatigue. It can also result in decreased productivity and creativity, as the mind and body are not given enough time to rest and recharge. Without a well-balanced work-life schedule, individuals may find themselves constantly working and feeling constantly stressed, which can negatively impact their overall quality of life. Neglecting personal life is another potential consequence of failing to establish a work-life balance. Pursuing a passion and turning it into a business can be incredibly rewarding, but it is important not to let it consume one's entire life. It is crucial to set aside time for activities and relationships outside of work in order to maintain a sense of fulfillment and connection to the world beyond one's hobbies. In addition to preventing burnout and neglecting personal life, establishing a work-life balance can also benefit the overall success of one's hobby-turned-business. By setting boundaries and creating a structured schedule, individuals can ensure that they are allocating time and energy to both work and personal life. This can enhance productivity and prevent the feeling of being overwhelmed. When individuals have time to rest and engage in activities outside of work, they are more likely to approach their work with a fresh perspective and renewed energy. They may also have more time to invest in self-improvement and skill development, further enhancing their expertise and marketability in their chosen field. By maintaining a healthy work-life balance, individuals can optimize their performance and increase their chances of long-term success. Establishing a work-life balance is essential for maintaining healthy relationships. Neglecting personal life in pursuit of a passion can strain relationships with friends, family and significant others. It is important to allocate time to spend with loved ones and engage in activities that nurture those relationships. By prioritizing personal connections and maintaining open communication with loved ones, individuals can ensure that their relationships remain strong and supportive. these relationships can also provide a valuable source of encouragement, motivation and perspective when faced with challenges or setbacks in the pursuit of monetizing hobbies.

While the pursuit of turning hobbies into a source of income can be exciting and fulfilling, it is crucial to establish a work-life balance in order to avoid overworking or neglecting personal life. By setting boundaries, prioritizing self-care and maintaining healthy relationships, individuals can prevent burnout, increase productivity and enhance their overall quality of life. It is through this harmonious integration of work and personal life that individuals can truly monetize their passion and find long-term success and fulfillment.

DEDICATING TIME TO PURSUE PERSONAL HOBBIES SEPARATE FROM THE BUSINESS

Dedicating time to pursue personal hobbies separate from the business is an essential aspect of turning your hobbies into income. While it is crucial to have a passion for your business, it is equally important to maintain a healthy work-life balance. By carving out specific time for personal hobbies, individuals can not only prevent burnout but also find inspiration and creativity that can be channeled into their business endeavors.

One of the main benefits of dedicating time to personal hobbies is the prevention of burnout. When individuals are deeply immersed in their business ventures, they often neglect their personal lives, which can lead to exhaustion and decreased productivity. By setting aside time to engage in activities unrelated to their business, individuals can recharge and rejuvenate themselves. For example, if someone has a passion for painting, they can allocate a specific time each day or week to work on their artwork. During this time, they can forget about the pressures and stresses of their business and focus solely on their hobby. This detachment allows individuals to take a break from their professional responsibilities and return to their work with a refreshed and energized mindset. Pursuing personal hobbies separate from the business can provide a rich source of inspiration. Engaging in activities outside of the business realm exposes individuals to new ideas, experiences and perspectives. These fresh perspectives can be incredibly valuable when it comes to problem-solving and generating innovative ideas for the business. For instance, someone who enjoys hiking may stumble upon a breathtaking view or encounter an unexpected obstacle during their expedition. These experiences can spark creativity and provide insights that can be applied to the business. By immersing themselves in personal hobbies, individuals open their minds to new possibilities that can fuel their entrepreneurial endeavors. Dedicating time to personal hobbies can serve as a source of creativity for business-related activities. Some hobbies require individuals to think outside the box and tap into their creative side. For example, playing a musical instrument demands the creation of melodies and harmonies, while writing requires weaving words together to form compelling narratives. These creative skills developed through personal hobbies can be transferred to the business realm, enabling individuals to approach their work with a unique and innovative perspective. By exploring personal passions, individuals can unlock their creative potential, leading to novel business ideas and strategies.

Personal hobbies can act as a form of stress relief, enhancing overall well-being. Engaging in activities that bring joy and relaxation is crucial for mental and emotional health. The demands of running a business can be overwhelming, with constant pressure to meet deadlines, handle client expectations and navigate unforeseen challenges. Personal hobbies offer individuals a respite from the stress and provide an outlet for self-expression and enjoyment. Whether it is gardening, cooking or playing a sport, engaging in activities that bring happiness and fulfillment can contribute to a person's overall well-being. In turn, this improved well-being translates into increased productivity and success in their business pursuits. Dedicating time to pursue personal hobbies separate from the business is a valuable practice to turn hobbies into income. It prevents burnout, fosters inspiration, fuels creativity and nurtures overall well-being. By allocating specific time for personal passions, individuals can strike a healthy work-life balance and unlock the full potential of their entrepreneurial pursuits. The integration of personal hobbies into one's business journey not only leads to financial success but also offers a more rewarding and fulfilling professional life.

Turning your hobbies into a source of income can be a dream come true for many people. Imagine being able to do what you love and make money from it. Fortunately, in today's digital age, there are numerous opportunities to monetize your passion. In this article, we will explore how to identify these opportunities, create a business plan and utilize digital tools to turn your hobbies into a sustainable source of income. The first step in monetizing your passion is to identify the opportunities that exist in the market. Take some time to research and analyze the demand for your particular hobby. Is there a large enough market to support your business? Are there other entrepreneurs already successfully monetizing the same hobby? Understanding the market landscape will help you identify any gaps or niches that you can potentially fill. Once you have identified the opportunities, it is crucial to create a business plan. A business plan serves as a roadmap for your venture and outlines your goals, target audience, marketing strategies and financial projections. It is essential to thoroughly research and develop a comprehensive plan that includes all the necessary steps to turn your hobby into an income-generating business. Digital tools have revolutionized the way we live and work and they can be instrumental in monetizing your passion. Social media platforms such as Instagram, YouTube and TikTok provide an excellent opportunity to showcase your skills and attract an audience. Utilize these platforms to create engaging content related to your hobby, which can include tutorials, behind-the-scenes footage or even personal stories that resonate with your audience. Building a strong online presence is a crucial step in monetizing your passion, as it helps you connect with potential customers and build a community around your brand. Another digital tool that can greatly benefit your business is a website or an online store. A well-designed website not only serves as a digital storefront for your products or services, but it also helps establish your credibility and professionalism. Your website should include a comprehensive description of your offerings, high-quality visuals and a seamless checkout process. Consider incorporating a blog or a portfolio section where you can showcase your expertise and attract potential clients. Remember to optimize your website for search engines to ensure that your target audience can easily find you online. In addition to social media platforms and websites, digital marketing tools such as email marketing, search engine optimization (SEO) and pay-per-click (PPC) advertising can significantly boost your online visibility and help you reach a wider audience. Email marketing allows you to build a loyal customer base by sending personalized newsletters, updates and promotions. SEO ensures that your website appears higher in search engine results, increasing your chances of being discovered by potential customers. PPC advertising, on the other hand, allows you to create targeted advertisements that appear alongside relevant search results or on social media platforms. By utilizing these tools strategically, you can maximize your online reach and increase your chances of success in monetizing your passion. While digital tools are essential in monetizing your hobby, never underestimate the power of networking and collaboration. Attend industry events, join online communities and connect with like-minded individuals who share your passion. Collaborating with others can help expand your reach and open doors to new opportunities. Consider partnering with other businesses or influencers who align with your brand to cross-promote each other's offerings and tap into a wider customer base. Turning your hobbies into a source of income is possible if you approach it strategically and utilize the digital tools available to you. Identify the opportunities that exist in your market, create a comprehensive business plan and leverage social media platforms, websites and digital marketing tools to build a strong online presence. Remember to network and collaborate with others in your industry to maximize your potential for success. By following these steps, you can transform your passion into a sustainable source of income and truly live the dream of doing what you love while making money from it.

X. CONCLUSION

Monetizing your passion and turning your hobbies into a source of income can be a fulfilling and profitable endeavor. Whether it is through selling handmade crafts, providing services in your area of expertise or creating digital content, there are numerous opportunities available for individuals to capitalize on their interests. It is important to approach this process with caution and thorough planning. Identifying viable opportunities is crucial, as not all hobbies may translate well into profitable ventures. Conducting market research and feasibility studies can help determine the demand for your product or service, assess competition and identify potential customers. Once you have identified a viable opportunity, creating a detailed business plan becomes imperative. This will help outline your goals, strategies and financial projections, providing a roadmap for your entrepreneurial journey. It is essential to consider factors such as pricing, target audience, marketing strategies and necessary resources. Incorporating digital tools into your business plan is essential in today's digital age. Utilizing social media platforms, online marketplaces and digital marketing techniques can significantly enhance your reach and visibility, enabling you to connect with a larger audience and generate more sales. It is important to continuously improve and adapt your business as you navigate the journey of monetizing your passion. Being open to feedback, learning from mistakes and staying updated with industry trends can help you stay ahead of the competition. Networking and building relationships with like-minded individuals or professionals can provide valuable insights, advice and opportunities for collaboration. It is important to remember that monetizing your passion requires dedication, hard work and perseverance. While it may seem enticing to be able to do what you love and make money from it, success does not come overnight. It is essential to have realistic expectations and be prepared for the challenges and uncertainties that may arise along the way. Building a successful business takes time, effort and a commitment to continuous improvement. It is crucial to strike a balance between pursuing your passion and maintaining your motivation. When your hobby becomes a means of income, it may be easy to lose sight of the joy and satisfaction it once brought you. It is important to create boundaries, schedule breaks and engage in activities that help you reconnect with your passion outside of work. Finding this balance will not only help you stay motivated but also prevent burnout and ensure the longevity of your business. The journey of monetizing your passion can be an exciting and rewarding one. By identifying viable opportunities, creating a comprehensive business plan, leveraging digital tools, continuously improving and adapting and maintaining a balance between work and passion, individuals can turn their hobbies into a sustainable source of income. It is important to approach this process with realistic expectations, dedication and perseverance. Success does not come overnight, but with diligence and a passion for what you do, the possibilities are endless. So, why not take the leap and turn your hobbies into a profitable venture? Discover the joy of doing what you love and making money from it today!

RECAP OF THE MAIN POINTS DISCUSSED IN THE ESSAY

This essay has explored the concept of turning hobbies into a source of income, providing a comprehensive guide on how to effectively monetize one's passions. Throughout the essay, several key points were discussed. It was highlighted that identifying opportunities is crucial in this process. Individuals are encouraged to evaluate their hobbies and determine if there is a demand for the products or services they can offer. It was emphasized that researching the market and understanding competitors is essential to ensure viability and success. Creating a business plan emerged as a vital step in the monetization journey. This plan requires careful consideration of financial aspects, such as budgeting and pricing strategies, as well as marketing and promotion strategies crucial to attracting customers. A business plan acts as a roadmap that guides individuals in their entrepreneurial journey, enabling them to set clear goals and objectives. The essay stressed the importance of utilizing digital tools in the process of monetizing one's passions. Digital platforms provide convenient and effective means of reaching a wide audience and establishing an online presence. Social media platforms, in particular, play a significant role in promoting products and services, engaging with potential customers and building a brand image. E-commerce platforms and websites allow individuals to sell their products or services directly, facilitating customer transactions and enhancing convenience. It is crucial to acknowledge the importance of continuous learning and skill development. Embracing new technologies, improving marketing strategies and staying updated with industry trends are essential to remain competitive in the evolving market. Individuals are encouraged to invest in their personal and professional growth by attending workshops, conferences or online courses relevant to their respective fields. Networking and collaborating with individuals in the same industry can provide valuable insights and opportunities for growth. The essay emphasized the significance of passion as the driving force towards success. The journey of monetizing hobbies may be challenging, requiring dedication, persistence and resilience. Individuals who are genuinely passionate about their interests are more likely to persevere through obstacles and setbacks. Passion not only motivates individuals to improve their skills and deliver high-quality products or services, but it also attracts customers who value authenticity. The importance of maintaining a balance between passion and profitability was highlighted. While turning hobbies into a source of income can be exciting, it is essential to avoid neglecting the initial love and enjoyment for the activity. Individuals are encouraged to find a harmonious balance between the creative aspect and the business aspect. This essay has provided a comprehensive overview of the process of monetizing hobbies. By identifying opportunities, creating a business plan, utilizing digital tools, continuously learning and developing skills, embracing passion and maintaining a balance, individuals can successfully turn their passions into a profitable venture. Monetizing hobbies provides not only financial benefits but also personal fulfillment, allowing individuals to do what they love and make money from it. By following the steps outlined in this essay, individuals can embark on an entrepreneurial journey that combines their passion with profitability, leading to a fulfilling and prosperous future.

REINFORCEMENT OF THE VALUE OF MONETIZING HOBBIES AND PASSIONS

Reinforcement of the value of monetizing hobbies and passions is crucial in today's society, as it offers individuals the opportunity to pursue their interests while also generating income. Many people are no longer content with working traditional nine-to-five jobs that provide little personal fulfillment. Instead, they seek to turn their hobbies and passions into viable business ventures, allowing them to do what they love while making a profit. By monetizing hobbies and passions, individuals can unlock a whole new realm of possibilities and potentially achieve financial success while maintaining a sense of personal fulfillment. One of the key benefits of monetizing hobbies and passions is the ability to merge work and leisure time. Unlike traditional jobs, which often restrict individuals to a specific set of tasks and hours, monetizing one's passion allows for flexibility and autonomy. For example, consider someone who enjoys photography and wants to turn it into a business. By monetizing their passion, they can set their own schedule, determine the types of photography they want to specialize in and work with clients who share their artistic vision. This not only allows for a more personalized and enjoyable work experience but also enhances overall job satisfaction. Monetizing hobbies and passions can also lead to increased creativity and innovation. When individuals are able to turn their passions into income-generating ventures, they are more motivated to innovate and push their boundaries. For instance, an individual who loves cooking may start a catering business but eventually expand their services to offer cooking classes or publish a recipe book. By monetizing their passion, they are encouraged to constantly explore new ideas and find ways to stand out in a competitive market. This drive for innovation can have a ripple effect, positively impacting other aspects of their lives and further fueling their creativity.

Monetizing hobbies and passions allows individuals to pursue multiple revenue streams. In today's digital age, there are numerous platforms and tools available for individuals to showcase their talents and reach a broader audience. For instance, a musician can generate income not only from live performances but also from selling digital music downloads, merchandise and even by monetizing their YouTube channel. By diversifying their income streams, individuals can maximize their potential earnings while also mitigating financial risks. This can provide a sense of financial security and stability, further validating the value of monetizing hobbies and passions. In addition to financial benefits, monetizing hobbies and passions can also have a positive impact on an individual's mental and emotional well-being. Research has shown that engaging in activities one is passionate about can reduce stress levels, increase happiness and improve overall mental health. Consequently, transforming these activities into income-generating ventures allows individuals to experience these benefits on a daily basis, rather than reserving them for their leisure time. By pursuing work that aligns with their passions, individuals can cultivate a genuine sense of purpose and fulfillment, leading to improved psychological well-being. To successfully monetize hobbies and passions, individuals must also understand the value of leveraging digital tools. In today's technology-driven world, having a strong online presence is essential for reaching potential customers and clients. Platforms such as social media, online marketplaces and e-commerce websites provide individuals with opportunities to showcase their work, attract customers and generate sales. By utilizing these digital tools, individuals can leverage the power of the internet to establish their brand, connect with a broader audience and ultimately monetize their hobbies and passions more effectively. The reinforcement of the value of monetizing hobbies and passions cannot be overstated. By turning one's passion into a source of income, individuals can merge work and leisure time, leading to increased job satisfaction. Monetizing hobbies and passions also fosters creativity and innovation, allowing individuals to constantly explore new opportunities and expand their business ventures. Diversifying income streams and leveraging digital tools can provide financial security and stability. Monetizing hobbies and passions contributes to overall mental and emotional well-being, as individuals can experience a sense of purpose and fulfillment through their work. By understanding and embracing the value of monetizing hobbies and passions, individuals can unlock their full potential and live a more fulfilling and prosperous life.

FINAL ENCOURAGEMENT TO TAKE STEPS TOWARDS TURNING HOBBIES INTO INCOME

It can also be daunting and overwhelming to take that leap of faith and turn your passion into a viable business. Nonetheless, with the right mindset and a strategic plan, you can successfully monetize your hobbies and create a sustainable source of income. The final encouragement lies in recognizing the immense potential and possibilities that lie ahead, as well as the many successful stories of individuals who have turned their hobbies into thriving businesses. First and foremost, it is essential to recognize the untapped opportunities that exist within your hobby. Take a step back and assess the market demand and potential customer base for your particular passion. Is there a gap that you can fill? Is there a unique spin or approach that you can bring to the table? By thoroughly understanding the needs and wants of your target audience, you can position your hobby as a solution or offering that others are willing to pay for. Once you have identified the opportunities, it is crucial to create a comprehensive business plan. This plan will serve as your roadmap, guiding you through the process of launching and growing your hobby-turned-business. Your business plan should include a clear mission statement, a detailed description of your offering, a market analysis, a marketing and sales strategy, financial projections and a plan for scaling and expanding your business in the future. By thoroughly planning and strategizing, you can set yourself up for success and mitigate potential risks or challenges along the way.

In today's digital age, there are countless digital tools and platforms that can help you monetize your passion. Whether it's setting up an online store, creating a website or leveraging social media channels, digital tools can significantly amplify your reach and impact. Engaging with your audience through online platforms not only allows you to showcase and sell your products or services but also enables you to build a community and establish yourself as an authority within your niche. Digital tools can help streamline your operations, allowing you to focus on what you love doing while automating the administrative tasks that come with running a business. While turning your hobbies into income may seem like a daunting task, it is important to remember the success stories that have come before you. There are countless examples of individuals who have turned their passions into lucrative businesses. From artists selling their artwork to food enthusiasts starting successful catering businesses, the possibilities are endless. By immersing yourself in the stories and experiences of others who have successfully monetized their passions, you can gain valuable insights, inspiration and motivation to take that leap of faith. Turning your hobbies into income is an exciting and fulfilling journey that requires determination, strategic planning and a willingness to learn and adapt. By recognizing the opportunities within your passion, creating a comprehensive business plan, leveraging digital tools and drawing inspiration from successful stories, you can turn your hobbies into a sustainable source of income. It may not be an easy path, but with passion, perseverance and a well-thought-out plan, you can make money doing what you love. So, take that leap of faith, embrace the challenges and uncertainties and embark on the rewarding journey of turning your hobbies into income.

BIBLIOGRAPHY

Simone C. O. Conceição. 'Creating a Sense of Presence in Online Teaching.' How to "Be There" for Distance Learners, Rosemary M. Lehman, John Wiley & Sons, 8/30/2010

Wolfgang Ulaga. 'Monetizing Data.' A Practical Roadmap for Framing, Pricing & Selling Your B2B Digital Offers, Stephan Liozu, Ulaga & Associés, 10/30/2018

Barbara Arena. 'The Complete Idiot's Guide to Making Money with Your Hobby.' Penguin, 1/1/2001

Philip Kotler. 'Kellogg on Marketing.' The Marketing Faculty of the Kellogg School of Management, Alexander Chernev, John Wiley & Sons, 4/5/2023

Orville C. Walker. 'Marketing Strategy.' A Decision-focused Approach, McGraw-Hill/Irwin, 1/1/2003

Jeremiah Thayer. 'Running a Food Hub: Volume Two, a Business Operations Guide.' James Matson, Government Printing Office, 9/17/2015

Sari Edelstein. 'Managing Food and Nutrition Services.' For the Culinary, Hospitality and Nutrition Professions, Jones & Bartlett Learning, 1/1/2008

James F. Sherman. 'Retirement Housing Markets.' Project Planning and Feasibility Analysis, Susan B. Brecht, J. Wiley, 1/1/1991

Xiao-lei Wang. 'Maintaining Three Languages.' The Teenage Years, Multilingual Matters, 11/5/2015

Ian Khan. 'Metaverse For Dummies.' John Wiley & Sons, 1/16/2023

Adolphine da Silva. 'Define your Business Goal.' Lulu Press, Inc, 9/16/2016

William A. Sahlman. 'How to Write a Great Business Plan.' Harvard Business Review Press, 3/1/2008

Dan S. Kennedy. 'The Ultimate Marketing Plan.' Target Your Audience! Get Out Your Message! Build Your Brand!, Simon and Schuster, 5/18/2011

Simon Hudson. 'Tourism and Hospitality Marketing.' A Global Perspective, SAGE, 2/18/2008

Shu Chen Hou. 'The Automated Money Machine: Build Your Online Empire for Passive Income.' Passive Income Made Easy!, Shu chen Hou, 7/8/2023

Srinivas R. Kandula. 'International Human Resource Management.' SAGE Publishing India, 7/31/2018

Kalpit Chaddha. 'How To Build a Profitable YouTube Channel.' Kalpit Chaddha, 3/10/2023

Russell Robb. 'Buying Your Own Business.' Bullets: * Identify Opportunities, * Analyze True Value, Negotiate the Best Terms, * Close the Deal, Simon and Schuster, 5/1/2008

Stanford M. Lyman. 'Civilization: Contents, Discontents and Malcontents and Other Essays (c).' University of Arkansas Press, 1/1/1990

Erin Cech. 'The Trouble with Passion.' How Searching for Fulfillment at Work Fosters Inequality, Univ of California Press, 10/26/2021

Rod Yochim. 'Guide To Launching Your Own E-Business.' How To Monetize Your Hobbies: Starting A Hobby Business, Amazon Digital Services LLC - KDP Print US, 9/19/2021

www.ingramcontent.com/pod-product-compliance
Lightning Source LLC
Chambersburg PA
CBHW072354290526
45794CB00001B/66